Investigating the Teacher's Life and Work

STUDIES IN PROFESSIONAL LIFE AND WORK
Volume 1

Scope
The series will commission books in the broad area of professional life and work. This is a burgeoning area of study now in educational research with more and more books coming out on teachers' lives and work, on nurses' life and work, and on the whole interface between professional knowledge and professional lives.

The focus on life and work has been growing rapidly in the last two decades. There are a number of rationales for this. Firstly, there is a methodological impulse: many new studies are adopting a life history approach. The life history tradition aims to understand the interface between people's life and work and to explore the historical context and the socio-political circumstances in which people's professional life and work is located. The growth in life history studies demands a series of books which allow people to explore this methodological focus within the context of professional settings.

The second rationale for growth in this area is a huge range of restructuring initiatives taking place throughout the world. There is in fact a world movement to restructure education and health. In most forms this takes the introduction of more targets, tests and tables and increasing accountability and performativity regimes. These initiatives have been introduced at governmental level – in most cases without detailed consultation with the teaching and nursing workforces. As a result there is growing evidence of a clash between people's professional life and work missions and the restructuring initiatives which aim to transform these missions. One way of exploring this increasingly acute clash of values is through studies of professional life and work. Hence the European Commission, for instance, have begun to commission quite large studies of professional life and work focussing on teachers and nurses. One of these projects – the Professional Knowledge Network project has studied teachers' and nurses' life and work in seven countries. There will be a range of books coming out from this project and it is intended to commission the main books on nurses and on teachers for this series.

The series will begin with a number of works which aim to define and delineate the field of professional life and work. One of the first books 'Investigating the Teacher's Life and Work' by Ivor Goodson will attempt to bring together the methodological and substantive approaches in one book. This is something of a 'how to do' book in that it looks at how such studies can be undertaken as well as what kind of generic findings might be anticipated.

Future books in the series might expect to look at either the methodological approach of studying professional life and work or provide substantive findings from research projects which aim to investigate professional life and work particularly in education and health settings.

Investigating the Teacher's Life and Work

Ivor Goodson
Education Research Centre,
University of Brighton, UK

SENSE PUBLISHERS
ROTTERDAM / TAIPEI

A C.I.P. record for this book is available from the Library of Congress.

ISBN 978-90-8790-408-1 (paperback)
ISBN 978-90-8790-409-8 (hardback)
ISBN 978-90-8790-410-4 (e-book)

Published by: Sense Publishers,
P.O. Box 21858, 3001 AW
Rotterdam, The Netherlands
http://www.sensepublishers.com

Printed on acid-free paper

CONTENTS

INTRODUCTION

Ivor Goodson

In the past decades there has been a reaction in most western countries to foundational disciplinary theory, such as philosophy of education or history of education. It has been thought that the disciplinary base of the theory leads researchers too far away from the practical world of the teacher.

As a result a number of counter-narratives have sought to re-enter the practitioner's world and, explore research in this milieu; genres such as teacher's stories, 'reflective practice' and action research are examples of such a move back to action and practice.

Nonetheless a survey of these genres reflects a common problem; in entering the teacher's practical world they have too often lost contact with the historical context of practice and with theoretical and disciplinary understanding generally. Thus, in trying to bring the teacher back into educational study they have had the paradoxical result of weakening the teacher's understanding of context, politics, patterns and theories. By entering the world of practice and evacuating these other zones they have in fact ended up 'domesticating' the teacher. By focusing at the end of the teaching process on action and on practice they have given up the task of understanding how actions and practice change historically and that they are socially and politically constructed in different ways at different times. Just as some work using action research and practical reflection domesticate the teacher, so also they domesticate the researcher.

What is urgently required are genres which stay close to the teacher's life-world and which systematically build the links to history, politics and theory. Stenhouse long ago argued that we need a 'story of action within a theory of context' and argued that historical methods could provide a base for such integration (L. Stenhouse, 1977, p. 7).

This book seeks to broaden the investigation of how to generate theory building. Since Stenhouse's death in 1982 a new genre of life history has been generated which has sought to explore the teacher's story of action in a historical context. This work allows us to concentrate on the teacher's life-world, but doing so in ways that allows us to explore political and social context and historical patterns and parameters.

We require a 'theory-building meeting ground' which brings together the work of the teacher's life-world with work on the thematic patterns and historical contexts of school life. The teacher's life history provides the personal grounding for investigation and the development of historical understanding allows a broader discussion of political and theoretical contexts.

New educational theory will change three aspects in particular:
- The context of investigations and substantive theory
- The form of presentation of research

– The 'meeting ground': in which action and theory are discussed and elaborated.

Life history and historical methods link the personal, the practical and the theoretical in new ways that operate at all three these levels.

Above all, these methods lead to developing theory in the 'middle ground': the arena between structural organization and policy of political contexts and the micro-detail of daily life in classrooms and teaching (see Goodson 1994). Middle ground theory seeks to combine the view from below with a focus on strategies and organizational forms that respond to changes in macro-level organizational structure and policy contexts. By focusing on the middle-ground substantive theories at that level can produce connections with daily teaching realities and - facing the other way - with formal theories of a structuralist and post-structuralist kind.

The following 2 chapters look at the use of life histories in the study of teaching, the sponsorship of teachers' voices and the forms of representation of teachers. The aim in these first 2 chapters is to present the argument for employing studies of life history in our understanding of teachers and teaching and further to review the various movements towards teacher narratives and teacher life histories. As has been explained these are very current movements in most western societies at the moment and must be read against a background of an increasing embrace of practical modes of understanding and a consequent movement away from disciplinary and theoretical discourses. The intention of life history study is to reposition, relocate and rejoin the world of action to the world of theory. It will be argued in this book that life history is a particularly fruitful way to reconnect action and theory in the contemporary educational world. In chapters 3 and 4 some guidelines for the conducting of life history interviews are presented. This is by no means an exhaustive list of the stages and procedures for life history interviews but it provides an introduction to those students and researchers beginning to use the method. Likewise the use of life story data is explored and some examples provided.

The provision of examples of life history work is very important for students and researchers approaching the life history method. Hence in chapter 5, 6, 7 examples of life history are employed. It is important to recognize that life history work is not only focused on the life history interview with the teacher but involves the recovery and analysis of a wide range of documentary sources together with the collection of other testimonies. In chapter 5 the product of some of this life history collection is presented in a portrayal of one particular teacher working in the United States in the 1990s. In Chapter 6 and 7 a more detailed use of life history data in building up a a picture of school life is presented.

The final chapter on life histories and professional practice provides some summary comments about investigating the teacher's life and work and shows how this data can expand our understanding of teachers and the world of schooling.

REFERENCES

Goodson, I. F. (1994). *Studying curriculum: Cases and methods.* Open University Press, Buckingham/Teachers College Press, New York/OISE Press, Toronto/probably in Australia by George Allen & Unwin.

Stenhouse, L. (1977). *Case study as a basis for research in a theoretical contemporary history of education.* Norwich: Centre for Applied Research in Education, University of East Anglia.

INVESTIGATING THE LIFE AND WORK OF TEACHERS

Ivor Goodson

THE TEACHER'S LIFE AND WORK

Studies of the teacher's life and work have increased and improved in recent decades. Writing in 1975, at the end of what Hobsbawm has called a 'golden age' for Western society (Hobsbawm, 1994), Lortie (1975) summarized the relationship between teachers and educational research studies in the US. Whilst those were very different economic and social times, his judgement stands up well today:

> Schooling is long on prescription, short on description. That is nowhere more evident than in the case of the two million persons who teach in the public schools. It is widely conceded that the core transactions of formal education take place where teachers and students meet. ... But although books and articles instructing teachers on how they should behave are legion, empirical studies of teaching work-and the outlook of those who staff the schools - remain rare. (p. vii)

In general, the point that Lortie makes has continued to be in force in the research discourse as related to teachers - a good deal of prescription and implicit portrayal but very little serious study of, or collaboration with, those prescribed to or portrayed. However, whilst there is continuity, there is also change over time which exists at the intersection of the educational enterprise with social, political and economic history.

A decade after Lortie, in the book *Teachers' Lives and Careers,* Ball and I (writing in 1985) argued that British research on teachers had moved through a number of contemporary phases in the last forty years. At the beginning of this period, in the 1960s,

> ... teachers were shadowy figures on the educational landscape mainly known, or unknown, through large scale surveys or historical analyses of their position in society, the key concept in approaching the practice of the teaching was that of role. (Ball & Goodson, 1985, p. 6)

Thus, in that decade in most research studies, teachers were present in aggregate through imprecise statistics or were viewed as individuals only as formal role incumbents, mechanistically and unproblematically responding to the powerful expectations of their role set.

By the late 1960s and early 1970s new approaches were well underway which sought to address some of the limitations of these paradigms. Case study researchers began to scrutinize schooling as a social process, focussing their work on the manner through which school pupils were 'processed.' 'The sympathies of the researchers lay primarily with the pupils, working class and female pupils in particular, who were the 'under dogs' in the classroom, teachers were the 'villains of the piece" (Ball & Goodson, 1985, p. 7). By the 1980s we saw a further shift where attention began to be directed 'to the constraints within which teachers work.

Teachers were transformed from villains to 'victims' and in some cases, 'dupes' of the system within which they were required to operate' (p. 7).

Crucially in terms of the orientation of this chapter, the latter characterization of teachers opened up the question of 'how teachers saw their work and their lives.' Writing in 1981, I argued that researchers had not confronted the complexity of the school teacher as an active agent making his or her own history. Researchers, even when they had stopped treating the teacher as numerical aggregate, historical footnote, or unproblematic role incumbent, still treated teachers as interchangeable types unchanged by circumstance or time. As a result new research methods were needed:

> The pursuit of personal and biographical data might rapidly challenge the assumption of interchangeability. Likewise, by tracing the teacher's life as it evolved over time - throughout the teacher's career and through several generations - the assumption of timelessness might also be remedied. *In understanding something so intensely personal as teaching it is critical we know about the person the teacher is.* Our paucity of knowledge in this area is a manifest indictment of the range of our sociological imagination. The life historian pursues the job from his (sic) own perspective, a perspective which emphasizes the value of the person's 'own story.' (Goodson, 1981, p. 69)

Unfortunately, whilst studies of teachers lives and careers now began to be more generally pursued in the educational research community, political and economic changes were moving sharply in the opposite direction, and this was reflected in the kind of studies undertaken. The development of patterns of political and administrative control over teachers have become enormous in the 1980s and 1990s. In terms of power and visibility in many ways this represents 'a return to the shadows' for teachers who face new curriculum guidelines (in some countries like New Zealand and Britain, an all-encompassing national curriculum), teacher assessment and accountability, a barrage of new policy edicts, and new patterns of school governance and administration.

NEW DIRECTIONS FOR STUDYING THE LIFE AND WORK OF TEACHING

Recent work by qualitative researchers suggests innovative and interesting ways to address the goal of understanding teachers' *personal practical knowledge* (Connelly & Clandinin, 1989). The addition of the personal aspect in this formulation is a positive development, hinting as it does at the importance of biographical and personal perspectives. Other traditions have focussed on the reflective practitioner, on teachers as researchers of their own practice, and on phenomenological approaches to practice. Personal experiences thus are linked irrevocably to practice. It is as if the teacher *is* her or his practice. For teacher educators, such specificity of focus is understandable, but broader perspectives might achieve even more, not solely in terms of understandings, but ultimately in ways that feed back into changes in practical knowledge, public policy, and intimately broader theoretical understandings.

There are similar reservations about the 'reflective teacher' or 'teacher as researcher' mode of teacher education. The 'teacher as researcher' approach suggests a number of problems. Stressing that the teacher becomes the researcher of his or her own practice appears to free the researcher in the academy from clear responsibility in this process. But in my view, such researchers have a primary but somewhat neglected responsibility for sponsoring and sustaining the teacher as researcher. Hence, new traditions are developing which oppose the notion that the focus of the teacher as researcher should be mainly upon practice.

In some ways, this focus on practice is the logical outcome of the 'teacher as researcher,' for its converse is the 'researcher as teacher.'

The work of teachers is politically and socially constructed. The parameters of what constitutes practice, whether biographical or political, range over a wide terrain. To narrow the focus to 'practice as defined' is to make the focus of research a victim of historical circumstances, particularly political forces. In many ways, 'the forces of the market,' as articulated by the politicians of the New Right, is seeking to turn the teacher's practice into that of a technician, a routinised and trivialized deliverer of a pre-designed package. To accept those definitions and to focus on 'practice' so defined is tantamount to accepting this ideology. By focussing on practice in a narrow way, the initiative for defining the research agenda passes to politicians and bureaucrats. Far more autonomous and critical research will be generated if the research community adopts wider lenses of inquiry for the teacher as researcher. We need then to move well beyond the grasp of what I have called elsewhere the 'practical fundamentalists' (Goodson, 1995b, p. 145).

The new traditions that seek to broaden the focus of work with teachers ranges from life history and biographical studies (Goodson 1981, 1988, 1992; Goodson & Walker, 1991), to collaborative biography (Butt, Raymond, McCue, & Yamagishi, 1992), to teacher's professional and micro political knowledge (Goodson & Cole, 1993; Russell & Munby, 1992), and through a wide range of interesting and innovative feminist work (Acker, 1989, 1994; Delhi, 1994; Smith, 1990). This work seeks to broaden the focus of teacher education and development to include the social and political, the contextual, and the collective.

In particular, life history studies seek to broaden the focus of work with teachers. This work takes the 'teacher as researcher' and 'action research' modes as valuable entry points, but it moves to broaden the immediate focus on practice and on individual classrooms. Life history work is *par excellence* qualitative work. The pioneering work of Thomas and Znaniecki (1927) and other proponents at the Chicago School in the 1920s and 1930s is part of the qualitative legacy. Subsequent work, notably by Dollard (1949) and Klockars (1975) has continued the tradition of American scholarship. In Britain, the work of Paul Thompson (1988) and his use of life histories to study aging has continued to rehabilitate and develop the life history tradition.

In teacher education and teacher development, much pioneering work has been undertaken. The work of Sikes, Measor, and Woods (1985) is helpful in developing our understanding of teachers' careers, as is the study, *Teachers Lives and Careers* (Ball & Goodson, 1985). The study by Hargreaves (1994b), *Changing Teachers, Changing Times,* adds a valuable contextual commentary to our understanding of the enormous global changes that are affecting the life and work of teachers.

Lawn (1990) has written powerfully about teachers' biographies and of how teachers' work has been rapidly restructured in England and Wales. The teacher, he argues, has moved from 'moral responsibility' - particularly with regard to curricular matters - to a narrow technical competence. Teaching in short has had its area of moral and professional judgment severely reduced. He summarizes recent changes in this way:

> In the biographies of many teachers is an experience of, and an expectation of, curriculum responsibility not as part of a job description, a task, but as part of the moral craft of teaching, the real duty. The post-war tradition of gradual involvement in curriculum responsibility at primary and second level was the result of the wartime breakdown of education, the welfare aspects of schooling and the post-war reconstruction in which teachers played a pivotal, democratic role. The role of teaching expanded as the teachers expanded the role. In its ideological form within this period, professional autonomy was created as an idea. As the post-war consensus finally collapsed and corporatism was demolished by Thatcherism, teaching was again to be reduced, shorn of its involvement in policy and managed more tightly. Teaching is to be reduced to 'skills,' attending planning meetings, supervising others, preparing courses and reviewing the curriculum. It is to be 'managed' to be more 'effective.' In effect the intention is to depoliticize teaching and to turn the teacher into an educational worker. Curriculum responsibility now means supervising competencies. (p. 389)

Likewise Susan Robertson (1993) has analysed teachers' work in the context of post-Fordist economies (see also Robertson, 2000, for a more extended analysis). She argues that again the teachers' professionalism has been drastically reconstructed and replaced by a wholly 'new professionalism.'

The new professionalism framework is one where the teacher as worker is integrated into a system where there is
- (i) no room to negotiate,
- (ii) reduced room for autonomy, and
- (iii) the commodity value of flexible specialism defines the very nature of the task.

> In essence, teachers have been severed from those processes which would involve them in deliberations about the future shape of their work. And while many teachers are aware that change is taking place and talk of the 'good old days,' few are aware of the potential profundity of that change even when it is happening in their midst. Clearly educators have been eclipsed by a core of interests from the corporate sector and selected interests co-opted in the corporate settlement. (Robertson, 1993)

These major restructurings of the work and life of teachers highlight the limitations of those methods which focus on the practical and personal worlds of teachers. Teachers' personal and practical reminiscences and commentaries relate to their work and practice. So such data in the new domain described by Lawn and Robertson will be primarily about work where moral and professional judgement plays less and less of a part. By focussing on the personal and practical, teacher data and stories are encouraged which forgo the chance to speak of other ways, other people, other times, and other forms of being a teacher. The focus of research methods solely on the personal and practical is then an abdication of the right to speak on matters of social and political construction. By speaking in this voice about personal and practical matters, the researcher and teacher both lose a voice in the moment of speaking. For the voice that has been encouraged and granted space in the public domain, in the realm of personal and practical, is the voice of technical competency, the voice of the isolated classroom practitioner, the voice of the worker whose work has been restructured and reconstructed.

In studying the teacher's life and work in a fuller social context, the intention is to develop insights, often in a grounded and collaborative manner, into the social construction of teaching. In this way, teachers' stories of action can be reconnected with 'histories of context.' Hence teacher stories, rather than passively celebrating the continual reconstruction of teaching, will move to develop understandings of social and political construction. It is a move from commentary on what *is* to cognition of what *might be.*

Studying the teacher's life and work as social construction provides a valuable lens for viewing the new moves to restructure and reform schooling. Butt et al. (1992) have talked about the 'crisis of reform' when so much of the restructuring and reformist initiatives depend on prescriptions imported into the classroom but developed as political imperatives elsewhere. These patterns of intervention develop from a particular view of the teacher, a view which practical genres of study often work to confirm.

> All their lives teachers have to confront the negative stereotypes 'teacher as robot, devil, angel, nervous Nellie' - foisted upon them by the American culture. Descriptions of teaching as a 'flat occupation with no career structure, low pay, salary increments unrelated to merit' have been paralleled with portrayals of teaching as 'one great plateau' where 'it appears that the annual cycle of the school year lulls teachers into a repetitious professional cycle of their own.'
>
> Within the educational community, the image of teachers as semi-professionals who lack control and autonomy over their own work and as persons who do not contribute to the creation of knowledge has permeated and congealed the whole educational enterprise. Researchers have torn the teacher out of the context of classroom, plagued her with various insidious effects (Hawthorne, novelty, Rosenthal, halo), parcelled out into discrete skills the unity of intention and action present in teaching practices. (p. 55)

In some ways the crisis of reform is a crisis of prescriptive optimism - a belief that what is politically pronounced and backed with armouries of accountability tests will actually happen (see later). But the data which will challenge these simplifications, data rooted in the teacher's life and work, will have to move beyond the currently popular 'practical' viewpoints to develop a broader

DEVELOPING A COUNTER-CULTURE: RATIONALES FOR STUDYING THE TEACHER'S LIFE AND WORK

The project of analysing the teacher's life and work grows from a belief that there is a need for a counter culture which will resist the tendency common in research studies to leave teachers 'in the shadows.' This counter culture could arise from a research mode that places the study of teachers and the sponsorship of 'teachers' voices' at the centre of the research action.

> The proposal I am recommending is essentially one of reconceptionalising educational research so as to assure that the teacher's voice is heard, heard loudly, heard articulately. (Goodson, 1991, p. 36)

Of course the sponsorship of teacher voices is a somewhat pious incantation and can be a perilous one if too selectively appropriated and employed. Hargreaves (1994 and 1996) has cogently inveighed against the dangers of researchers choosing teacher voices that they are sympathetic with and silencing other voices. This is always, of course, a danger in research and nowhere more so than with a research modality that seeks to empower other voices. Nonetheless, the argument of Butt et al. (1992) carries the important aspiration of employing teachers' voices so that the danger of selectivity and appropriation can be faced:

> The notion of the teacher's voice is important in that it carries the tone, the language, the quality, the feelings, that are conveyed by the way a teacher speaks or writes. In a political sense the notion of the teacher's voice

addresses the right to speak and be represented. It can represent both the unique individual and the collective voice; one that is characteristic of teachers as compared to other groups. (p. 57)

The important point in this quote is the counter-cultural potential of teachers' knowledge standing against the grain of power and knowledge as held, produced, and promulgated by the politicians and administrators who control the educational systems.

Whilst it may seem to some that the current dominance of the New Right provides an unhealthy climate, and indeed seems unlikely to provide support for long-subordinated voices, on the other side, the postmodernist movement provides a series of supports for such development. Carol Gilligan's excellent work, *In a Different Voice,* shows the power of representing the voices of women previously unheard. Above all, new post-modern syntagmas sponsor 'the idea that all groups have a right to speak for themselves, in their own voice, and have that voice accepted as authentic and legitimate' (Harvey, 1989, p. 48).

As well as the general sponsorship of teachers' voices, there are a number of specific rationales for studying the teacher's life and work. Firstly, these kinds of studies provide a wide range of insights about the new moves to restructure and reform schooling. These new initiatives have been widely promoted, but they have seldom been viewed through the lens of the teacher's life and work. From this point of view, it is often meaningful to talk about a crisis of reform – or more specifically a crisis of prescription - for the new reforms and prescriptions often work, against the history and context of the teacher's life and work and by not listening to these concerns, new crises are generated. I have recently examined the salience of the belief in curriculum as prescription, but these comments could so easily be generalized into a more serious concern about new reform initiatives.

Curriculum as prescription (CAP) supports the mystique that expertise and control reside within central governments, educational bureaucracies or the university community. Providing nobody exposes this mystique, the two words of 'prescriptive rhetoric' and 'schooling as practice' can co-exist. Both sides benefit from such peaceful coexistence. The agencies of CAP are seen to be 'in control' and the schools are seen to be 'delivering' (and can carve out a good degree of autonomy if they accept the rules).

However there is a substantial downside to this 'historic compromise' which has a vital implication for the questions associated with teachers' voices.

There are costs of complicity in accepting the myth of prescription: above all these involve, in various ways, acceptance of established modes of power relations. Perhaps most importantly the people intimately connected with the day-to-day social construction of curriculum and schooling - teachers - are thereby effectively disenfranchised in the 'discourse of schooling.' To continue to exist, teachers' day-to-day power must remain unspoken and unrecorded. This is one price of complicity: day-to-day power and autonomy for schools and for teachers are dependent on continuing to accept the fundamental lie. (Goodson, 1990, p.300).

In addressing the crisis of prescription and reform, it becomes imperative that we find new ways to sponsor teachers' voices.

As a generative example, Casey's (1992) work provides an illustration of studying teachers' lives to understand the much discussed question of 'teacher drop-out.' She notes that a certain set of taken- for-granted assumptions control the way in which the problem of teacher attrition has normally been defined - one which presumes managerial solutions - and how the language confirms this direction by referring to 'teacher defection,' 'teacher turnover,' and 'supply and demand.' Hence, the question of teacher dropout is pushed into certain investigative cul-de-sacs through both the taken-for-granted assumptions and the linguistic phrasing which helps constitute the problem.

This capacity to direct investigations in particular directions and in ways that underpin managerialism and prescription is often confirmed by the research methods employed within the academy. Casey, for example, finds that former members of the teaching profession have often been traced statistically, rather than in person, and that information has typically been collected from sources such as district files, state departments of public instruction, or through researcher-conceived surveys. These strategies often work with the grain of power and knowledge as held by managers and the elites which surround the educational systems. Casey argues that,

> The particular configuration of selectivities and omissions which has been built into this research frame slants the shape of its findings. By systematically failing to record the voices of ordinary teachers, the literature on educators' careers actually silences them. Methodologically, this means that even while investigating an issue where decision making is paramount, researchers speculate on teachers' motivations, or at best, survey them with a set of forced-choice options. Theoretically, what emerges is an instrumental view of teachers, one in which they are reduced to objects which can be manipulated for particular ends.

> Politically, the results are educational policies constructed around institutionally convenient systems of rewards and punishments, rather than in congruence with teachers' desires to create significance in their lives. (Casey, 1992, p. 188)

Thus, a vital importance of teachers' voices and testimonies is that they expose the shallowness, not to say falsify, the managerial, prescriptive view of schooling. Hence, it is simple to see why it is that teachers' voices have been so long suppressed and in whose interests some academics have embraced certain research modes.

Secondly, another rationale for studying the life and work of teaching relates to the literature on teacher socialization. A major research theme in this literature has designated the period of pre-service teaching training and early phases of in-service training as the most formative socializing influence in the life and work of teaching. However, an alternative research tradition has insisted with accelerating force that the matter is far more complex. Many studies in the 1970s through to the 1990s have focused on teachers' own experiences as pupils.

Such early experiences are seen not only as important as the training periods but, in many cases, far more important. Dan Lortie (1975) has referred to this pupil period as an 'apprenticeship of observation' where teachers' observation and internalization many future role possibilities. Teacher socialization in this manner occurs through the observation and internalization of particular models of teaching experienced as the recipient people. Dan Lortie argues that these models, what he calls 'latent models,' are activated, not implanted, during the training period having often been 'carried in suspension,' so to speak, through the interim period of time. To explore seriously this alternative view of teacher socialization requires that we do more life history work covering the pattern of socialization of teachers over the full span of their life and work in teaching.

Yet another vital reason for studying the life and work of teaching arises from feminist studies, most particularly the exciting work of Acker and Middleton.

Their work and other feminist studies provide vital and insightful studies into teaching as a gendered profession (Acker, 1989, 1994; Middleton, 1992). Other specific studies have pursued the issue of women's life and work in teaching: for instance, Margaret Nelson's (1992) attempt to reconstruct the work experiences of women teachers in Vermont in the early twentieth century is a particularly important indication of the life history approach to studying the teacher's life and work. She notes:

> Numerous studies have shown that there is a gap between what we can discover when we rely on published accounts of some historical event and what we can discover when we ask questions of the on-site participants of those same events. This gap looms larger when we are looking at women's history because of the private nature of so much of women's lives. (Nelson, 1992, p. 168)

She adds later, 'Public history often ignores minority views. But women's lives are further hidden because important information is overlooked, consciously avoided, or distorted' (Nelson, 1992, p. 185).

Sue Middleton has cogently argues that 'writing one's autobiography becomes, in this framework, in part a process of deconstructing the discursive practices through which one's subjectivity has been constituted' (Middleton, 1992, p. 20). In this sense, her argument leads into a further rationale for studying the life and work of teaching, which in a sense is associated with the earlier section about managerialism and prescription. Our studies of the life and work of teaching should help produce a wider range of teacher-centred professional knowledge. I have pursued this argument at length elsewhere but, put briefly, the issue is how to develop a modality of educational research which speaks both of and to the teacher (Goodson, 1991, 1992, Goodson and Sikes 2001, Goodson 2005). To move our educational research study in this direction, we will require a major upheaval and reconceptualising of educational research paradigms. However, the emerging work from a range of genres from teacher thinking, through to teacher journaling, the teacher's professional knowledge, as well as the emerging corpus of work on reflective practitioners and action research is a solid starting point for a newly reconceptualized mode of educational research, as well as a basis for a new form of teacher professionalism (see Goodson & Hargreaves, 1996).

STUDYING TEACHERS' LIVES AND CAREERS

Studies of the teacher's life and work develop structural insights which locate the teacher's life within the deeply structured and embedded environments of schooling. The arguments for employing data on teachers' lives are substantial, but given the predominance of existing paradigms should be spelt out:

> In the research on schools in which I have been involved - covering a wide range of different research foci and conceptual matrixes – the consistency[1] of teachers talking about their own lives in the process of explaining their policies and practices has been striking. Were this only a personal observation it would be worthless, but again and again in talking to other researchers they have echoed their point. To give one example, David Hargreaves (Hargreaves, Hester, & Mellor, 1975), in researching for *Deviance in Classrooms,* noted that again and again teachers had imported autobiographical comments into their explanations. He was much concerned in retrospect by the speed with which such data had been excised when writing up the research. The assumption, very much the conventional wisdom, was that such data was too 'personal,' too 'idiosyncratic', too 'soft' for a fully fledged piece of social science research (Goodson, 1981).

Of course in the first instance (and in some cases the last instance) it is true that personal data can be irrelevant, eccentric, and essentially redundant. But the point that needs to be grasped is that these features are not the inevitable corollary of that which is personal. Moreover that which is personal at the point of collection may not remain personal. After all a good deal of social science is concerned with the collection of a range of often personal insights and events and the elucidation of more collective and generalizable profferings and processes.

The respect for the autobiographical, for 'the life,' is but one side of a concern to elicit the teachers' voice. In some senses, like other forms of good ethnographic investigation, this form of qualitative educational research is concerned to listen to what the teacher says and to respect and deal seriously with that data which the teacher imports into accounts. This, then, inverts the balance of proof. Conventionally those data which do not service the researcher's interests and foci are junked. In this model, the data the teacher provides has a more sacred property and is only dispensed with after painstaking proof of irrelevance and redundancy.

Listening to the teacher's voice should teach us that the autobiographical, 'the life,' is of substantial concern when teachers talk of their work. And at a commonsensical level, I find this essentially unsurprising. What I do find surprising, if not frankly unconscionable, is that for so long some researchers have ruled this part of the teacher's account out as irrelevant data.

Life experiences and background are obviously key ingredients of the person that we are, of our sense of self. To the degree that we invest our 'self in our teaching, experience and background therefore shape our practice.

A common feature in many teachers' accounts of their background is the appearance of a favourite teacher who substantially influenced the person as a young school pupil. Such teachers often report that 'it was this person who first sold me on teaching' or that 'I was sitting in her classroom when I first decided I wanted to be a teacher.' In short, such people provide a 'role model' and presumably influence the subsequent vision of desirable pedagogy as well as possible choice of subject specialism.

Many other ingredients of background are important in the teacher's life and practice. An upbringing in a working class environment may, for instance, provide valuable insights and experience when teaching pupils from a similar background. I once observed a teacher with a working class background teach a class of comprehensive pupils in a school in the East End of London. He taught using the local cockney vernacular, and his affinity was a quite startling aspect of his success as a teacher. In my interview I spoke about his affinity, and he noted that it was 'coz I come from round 'ere, don't I?' Background and life experience were, then, a major aspect of his practice. But so they would be in the case of middle class teachers teaching children from the working class or teachers of working class origins teaching middle class children. Background is an important ingredient in the dynamic of practice (see Lortie, 1975).

Of course, whilst class, gender, and ethnicity are but part of the larger picture, teachers' backgrounds and life experiences are idiosyncratic, unique, and must be explored therefore in their full complexity. Treatment of gender issues has often been historically inadequate (see Sikes et al, 1985). Recent work is more encouraging - see Nelson (1992), Smith (1990), Casey (1992), and Middleton (1992).

The teacher's *life style,* both in and outside school, his or her latent identities and cultures, impact on views of teaching and on practice. Becker and Geer's (1971) work on latent identities and cultures provide a valuable theoretical basis.

Life style is of course often a characteristic element in certain cohorts; for instance, work on the generation of 1960s teachers would be of great value in studying professionals who came in with profound and particular commitments to education as a vehicle for social change and social justice. In a recent study of a teacher focussing on his life style, Walker and I stated:

How the connections between youth culture and the curriculum reform movement of the sixties is more complex than we first thought. For Ron Fisher there definitely is a connection, he identifies strongly with youth culture and feels that to be important in his teaching. But despite his attraction to rock music and teenage life styles it is the school he has become committed to, almost against his own sense of direction. Involvement in innovation, for Ron at least, is not simply a question of technical involvement, but touches significant facets of his personal identity. This raises the question for the curriculum developer, what would a project look like if it explicitly set out to change the teachers rather than the curriculum? How would you design a project to appeal to the teacher-as-person rather than to the teacher-as-educator? What would be the effects and consequences of implementing such a design? (Goodson & Walker, 1991, p. 145)

This I think shows how work in this area begins to force a reconceptualization of models of teacher development. We move in short from the teacher-as practice to the teacher-as-person as our starting point for development.

The teachers' *lifecycle* is an important aspect of professional life and development.

This is a unique feature of teaching. For the teacher essentially confronts 'ageless' cohorts. This intensifies the importance of the lifecycle for perceptions and practices.

Focus on the *lifecycle* will generate insights into many of the unique elements of teaching. Indeed so unique a characteristic would seem an obvious starting point for reflection about the teachers' world. Yet our research paradigms face so frankly in other directions that there has been little work to date in this area.

Fortunately work in other areas provides a very valuable framework. Some of Gail Sheehy's somewhat populist work in *Passages* (1976), *Pathfinders* (1981) and *New Passages* (1995) is I think important. So also is the research work on which some of her publications are based carried out by Levinson. His work, whilst regrettably focussed only on men, does provide some generative insights into how our perspectives at particular stages in our life crucially effect our professional work. (For women's lives see new work just published by Levinson, 1996.)

Take for instance the case study of John Barnes, a university biologist. Levinson is writing about his 'dream' of himself as a front-rank prize-winning biological researcher:

Barnes's Dream assumed greater urgency as he approached 40. He believed that most creative work in science is done before then. A conversation with his father's lifelong friend around this time made a lasting impression on him. The older man confided that he had by now accepted his failure to become a 'legal star' and was content to be a competent and respected tax lawyer. He had decided that stardom is not synonymous with the good life; it was 'perfectly all right to be second best.' At the time, however, Barnes was not ready to scale down his own ambition. Instead, he decided to give up the chairmanship and devote himself fully to his research.

He stepped down from the chairmanship as he approached 41, and his project moved into its final phase. This was a crucial time for him, the culmination of years of striving. For several months, one distraction after another claimed his attention and heightened the suspense. He became the father of a little boy, and that same week was offered a prestigious chair at Yale. Flattered and excited, he felt that this was his 'last chance for a big offer.' But in the end Barnes said no. He found that he could not make a change at this stage of his work. Also, their ties to family and friends, and their love of place, were now of much greater importance to him and Ann. She said: 'The kudos almost got him, but now we are both glad we stayed.' (Levinson, 1979, p. 267)

This quotation I think shows how definitions of our professional location and of our career direction can only be arrived at by detailed understanding of people's lives. Studies of professional life and patterns of professional development must address this dimensions of the personal.

Likewise, *career stages* and *career decisions* can be analysed in their own right. Work on teachers' lives and careers is increasingly commanding attention in professional development workshops and courses. For instance, the Open University in England now uses our *Teachers Lives and Careers* (Ball & Goodson, 1985) book as one of its course set book. This is a small indication yet symptomatic of important changes in the way that professional courses are being reorganized to allow concentration on the perspective of teachers' careers.

Besides the selection of career studies in *Teachers Lives and Careers,* a range of new research is beginning to examine this neglected aspect of teachers' professional lives. The work of Sikes et al., (1985) has provided valuable new insights into how teachers construct and view their careers in teaching. More recent work on women's lifestyles to add to earlier work on men's life stages will help new studies in this area (see Levinson, 1979, 1996).

Moreover, work on teachers' careers points to the fact that there are *critical incidents* in teacher's lives and specifically in their work which may crucially affect perception and practice. Certainly work on beginning teachers has pointed to the importance of certain incidents in moulding teachers' styles and practices (see Lortie, 1975).

Other work on critical incidents in teachers' lives can confront important themes contextualised within a full life perspective. David Tripp's (1994) recent work provides a range of elegant examples of critical incident studies. Also, Kathleen Casey has employed 'life history narratives' to understand the phenomenon of teacher drop-out, specifically female and activist teacher dropout (Casey, 1988, 1992; Casey & Apple, 1989). Her work helps to understand this phenomenon which is currently receiving a great deal of essentially uncritical attention given the problem of teacher shortages. Yet few of the countries at the hard edge of teacher shortages have bothered to fund serious study of teachers' lives to examine and extend our understanding of the phenomenon of teacher drop-outs. I would argue that only such an approach affords the possibility of extending our understanding, and this is particularly important when new initiatives, such as those suggested by the Labour Party in the U.K., seek to bring back teachers who are over 50 into the profession.

Likewise with many other major themes in teachers' work. The question of teacher stress and bum-out would, I believe, be best studied through life history perspectives. Similarly the issue of effective teaching and the question of the take-up innovations and new managerial initiatives. Above all, in the study of teachers' working conditions, this approach has a great deal to offer.

Studies of teachers' lives might allow us to see the individual in relation to the history of her or his time, allowing us to view the intersection of the life history with the history of society thus illuminating the choices, contingencies, and options open to the individual. 'Life histories' of schools, subjects, and the teaching profession would provide vital contextual background in this respect. The initial focus on teachers' lives, therefore, would reconceptualize our studies of schooling and curriculum in quite basic ways (see Goodson, 1991, 1995a).

These different approaches to studying teachers' lives may seem too linear and logical for some current post-modern fashions. They might then be attacked from one of the more fashionable post-modern positions for their desire to provide coherence and closure to disparate and diverse lives in teaching. Such fashionable post-modernisms flow easily from the pens of some academics who study teachers, especially those who have never taught in school. But such persons look in the wrong place for the' closure' of teachers' lives - our academic discourses are not the main place that closure takes place, much as we might want to believe in their centrality.

Teachers' lives are subject to degrees of closure because they take place in one of the most historically circumscribed of social spaces. Schools are subject to a battery of government regulations, edicts, tests, accountabilities, and assessments-these provide parameters for the actions of teachers. Further, teachers are subject to systematic and invasive socialization during their education as well as pre-service and in-service training. The circumscription of space and the systemic nature of socialization are what predominantly 'frame' and 'close' teachers' lives.

So to follow post-modern fashion and see teachers as having 'selves' that are free-floating and multiple, subject to constant flux and change, ignores the circumscribed spaces and socialized trajectories of teachers' lives. Strategies for self-formation therefore take place in juxtaposition to the institutionalized and socialized practices of schooling. By focussing our study on the teacher's life and work in such closely patrolled institutional arenas, the intention, far from seeking academic closure, is on the contrary to create space for reflexivity. Such work aims to develop strategies for teachers to scrutinize and analyse their world of work - their lives in teaching - in ways that offer as flexible and informed a response to the socially constructed world of schooling as is possible.

NOTES

[1] The question of whether to use 'the teacher's voice' as a generic category or 'teachers' voices' is of more than semantic import. For any voice is multi-faceted whilst singularly embodied and embedded.

REFERENCES

Acker, S. (Ed.). (1989). *Teachers, gender and careers.* London, New York, and Philadelphia: Falmer Press.

Acker, S. (1994). *Gendered experience.* Milton Keynes: Open University Press.

Ball, S., & Goodson, I. F. (Eds.). (1985). *Teachers' lives and careers.* London, New York, and Philadelphia: Falmer Press.

Becker, H. S., & Geer, B. (1971). Latent culture: A note on the theory of latent social roles. In B. R. Cosin, et al. (Ed.), *School and society: A sociological reader* (pp. 56–60). London: Routledge & Kegan Paul.

Butt, R., Raymond, D., McCue, G., & Yamagishi, L. (1992). Collaborative autobiography and the teacher's voice. In I. F. Goodson (Ed.), *Studying teachers' lives* (pp. 51–98). London: Routledge.

Casey, K. (1988). *Teacher as author: Life history narratives of contemporary women teachers working for social change.* Doctoral dissertation. Madison: University of Wisconsin.

Casey, K. (1992). Why do progressive women activists leave teaching? Theory, methodology and politics in life history research. In I. F. Goodson (Ed.), *Studying teachers' lives* (pp. 187–208). London: Routledge.

Casey, K., & Apple, M. W. (1989). Gender and the conditions of teachers' work: The development of understanding in America. In S. Acker (Ed.), *Teachers, gender and careers.* London, New York and Philadelphia: Falmer Press.

Connelly, M., & Clandinin, J. (1989). *Teachers as curriculum planners.* New York: Teachers College Press.

Delhi, K. (1994). Subject to the new global economy: Power and positioning in Ontario labour market policy formation. In R. Priegert Coulter & I. F. Goodson (Eds.), *Rethinking vocationalism: Whose work/life is it?* (pp. 11141). Toronto: Our Schools/Ourselves.

Dollard, J. (1949). *Criteria for the life history.* New Haven, CT: Yale University Press.

Goodson, I. F. (1981). Life history and the study of schooling. *Interchange* (Ontario Institute for Studies in Education), *11*(4), 62–76.

Goodson, I. F. (1988). *The making of curriculum: Collected essays* (1st ed.). London, New York, & Philadelphia: Falmer Press.

Goodson, I. F. (1990). Studying curriculum: Towards a social constructionist perspective. *Journal of Curriculum Studies, 22*(4), 299–312.

Goodson, I. F. (1991). Sponsoring the teacher's voice: Teachers' lives and teacher development. *Cambridge Journal of Education, 21*(1), 35–45.

Goodson, I. F. (Ed.). (1992). *Studying teachers' lives.* London/New York/Toronto: Routledge/Teachers College Press/OISE Press.

Goodson, I. F. (1995a). Teachers, life histories and studies of curriculum and schooling. In I. F. Goodson (Ed.), *The making of curriculum: Collected essays* (2nd ed., pp. 71–92). London: Falmer.

Goodson, I. F. (1995b). Education as a practical matter: Some issues and concerns. *Cambridge Journal of Education, 25*(2), 137–147.

Goodson, I. F. (2005). *Learning, curriculum and life politics: The selected works of Ivor F. Goodson.* Routledge: Abingdon.

Goodson, I. F., & Cole, A. (1993). Exploring the teacher's professional knowledge. In D. McLaughlin & B. Tierney (Eds.), *Naming silenced lives* (pp. 71–94). London and New York: Routledge.

Goodson, I. F., & Hargreaves, A. (Eds.). (1996). *Teachers' professional lives.* London, New York and Philadelphia: Falmer Press.

Goodson, I. F., & Sikes. (2001). *Life history research in educational settings: Learning from live.* Buckingham and Philadelphia: Open University Press.

Goodson, I. F., & Walker, R. (1991). *Biography, identity and schooling: Episodes in education research.* London, New York and Philadelphia: Falmer Press.

Hargreaves, A. (1994a, April). *Dissonant voices: Teachers and the multiple realities of restructuring.* Paper presented at the annual meeting of the American Educational Research Association, New Orleans.

Hargreaves, A. (1994b). *Changing teachers, changing times.* Toronto/New York: Ontario Institute for Studies in Education Press/Teachers College Press.

Hargreaves, A. (1996). Revisiting voice. *Educational Researcher, 25*(1), 12–19.

Hargreaves, D. H., Hester, S., & Melior, F. (1975). *Deviance in classrooms.* London: Routledge & Kegan Paul.

Harvey, D. (1989). *The condition of post modernity: An enquiry into the origins of cultural change.* Oxford: Basil Blackwell.

Hobsbawm, E. (1994). *Age of extremes: The short twentieth century, 1914–1991.* London: Michael Joseph.

Klockars, C. B. (1975). *The professional fence.* London: Tavistock Publications.

Lawn, M. (1990). From responsibility to competency: A new context for curriculum studies in England and Wales. *Journal of Curriculum Studies, 22*(4), 388–392.

Levinson, D. J. (1979). *The seasons of a man's life.* New York: Ballantine Books.

Levinson, D. I., & Levinson, J. D. (1996). *The seasons of a woman's life.* New York: Alfred A. Knopf.

Lortie, D. (1975). *Schoolteacher: A sociological study.* Chicago: University of Chicago Press.

Middleton, S. (1992). Developing a radical pedagogy: Autobiography of a New Zealand sociologist of women's education. In I. F. Goodson (Ed.), *Studying teachers 'lives* (pp. 18–50). London: Routledge.

Nelson, M. (1992). Using oral histories to reconstruct the experiences of women teachers in Vermont, 1900–1950. In I. F. Goodson (Ed.), *Studying teachers 'lives* (pp. 167–186). London: Routledge.

Robertson, S. (1993). *Teachers' labour and post-Fordism: An exploratory analysis (mimeo).* Perth, Western Australia: Edith Cowan University.

Robertson, S. (2000). *A class act: Changing teachers' work, globalisation and the state.* New York: Garland/Falmer.

Russell, T., & Munby, H. (Ed.). (1992). *Teachers and teaching from classroom to reflection.* London, New York and Philadelphia: Falmer Press.

Sikes, P., Measor, L., & Woods, P. (1985). *Teachers' careers.* London, New York and Philadelphia: Falmer Press.

Sheehy, G. (1976). *Passages: Predictable crises in adult life.* New York: Dutton.

Sheehy, G. (1981). *Pathfinders.* London: Sidgwick & Jackson.

Sheehy, G. (1995). *New passages: Mapping your life across time.* Toronto: Random House of Canada.

Smith, D. E. (1990). *Conceptual practices of power: A feminist sociology of knowledge.* Toronto: University of Toronto Press.

Thomas, W. I., & Znaniecki, F. (1927). *The polish peasant in Europe and America* (2nd ed.). Chicago: University of Chicago Press.

Thompson, P. (1988). *The voices of the past: Oral history* (2nd ed.). Toronto: Oxford University Press.

Tripp, D. (1994). Teachers' lives, critical incidents, and professional practice. *International Journal of Qualitative Studies in Education, 7*(1), 65–76.

CHAPTER 2

THE USE OF LIFE HISTORIES IN THE STUDY OF TEACHING

Ivor Goodson

ORIGINS OF THE LIFE HISTORY METHOD

The first life histories, in the form of autobiographies of Native American chiefs, were collected by anthropologists at the beginning of the century. For sociologists the major landmark in the development of life history methods came two decades later with the publication of Thomas and Znaniecki's mammoth study The Polish Peasant in Europe and America (Thomas and Znaniecki, 1927). In exploring the experience of Polish peasants migrating to the United States, Thomas and Znaniecki relied mainly on the autobiographical accounts, diaries and letters provided by the migrants themselves. For these authors, life histories were the data par excellence of the social scientist:

> In analysing the experiences and attitudes of an individual, we always reach data and elementary facts which are not exclusively limited to this individual's personality, but can be treated as mere incidences of more or less general classes of data or facts, and can thus be used for the determination of laws of social becoming. Whether we draw our materials for sociological analysis from detailed life records of concrete individuals or from the observation of mass phenomena, the problems of sociological analysis are the same. But even when we are searching for abstract laws, life records, as complete as possible, constitute the *perfect* type of sociological material, and if social science has to use other materials at all it is only because of the practical difficulty of obtaining at the moment a sufficient number of such records to cover the totality of sociological problems, and of the enormous amount of work demanded for an adequate analysis of all the personal materials necessary to characterise the life of a social group. If we are forced to use mass phenomena as material, or any kind of happenings taken without regard to the life histories of the individuals who participated, it is a defect, not an advantage, of our present sociological method (pp.1831-1833).

Thomas and Znaniecki's pioneering work established the life history as a *bona fide* research device. The prominent position of the life history was further consolidated by the flourishing tradition of sociological research stimulated at Chicago by Robert Park. In the range of studies of city life completed under Park, *The Gang* (Thrasher, 1928), *The Gold Coast and the Slum* (Zorbaugh, 1929), *The Hobo*

(Anderson, 1923), and *The Ghetto* (Wirth, 1928), the life history method was strongly in evidence. Life history studies reached their peak in the 1930's with publications such as Clifford Shaw's account of a 'mugger' in *The Jack-Roller* (Shaw, 1930) and Edwin Sutherland's *The Professional Thief* (Cornwell and Sutherland 1937). Howard Becker's (1970) comments on Shaw's study underline one of the major strengths of the life history method:

> By providing this kind of voice from a culture and situation that are ordinarily not known to intellectuals generally and to sociologists in particular, *The Jack Roller* enables us to improve our theories at the most profound level: by putting ourselves in Stanley's skin, we can feel and become aware of the deep biases about such people that ordinarily permeate our thinking and shape the kinds of problems we investigate. By truly entering into Stanley's life, we can begin to see what we take for granted (and ought not to) in designing our research – what kinds of assumptions about delinquents, slums and Poles are embedded in the way we set the questions we study (Becker, 1970, p.71).

From this statement Becker leads on to the assertion that Stanley's story offers the possibility 'to begin to ask questions about delinquency from the point of view of the delinquent'. So that it follows that:

> If we take seriously, as his story must impel us to do, we might well raise a series of questions that have been relatively little studied – questions about the people who deal with delinquents, the tactics they use, their suppositions about the world, and the constraints and pressures they are subject to (p.71).

Becker's claims for the life history merely reiterate those made by contemporaries of the Chicago sociologists in the 1930's. Perhaps the best attempt to analyse the methodological base of the life history method was Dollard's *Criteria for the Life History* (Dollard, 1949). Foreshadowing Becker he argued that 'detailed studies of the lives of individuals will reveal new perspectives on the culture as a whole which are not accessible when one remains on the formal cross sectional plane of observation' (p.4). A central problem with Dollard however is his recurrent assertion, in the fashion of the times that the individual appears as a microcosm of the group features of the culture. This is a view, which as we shall see later is difficult to sustain. Yet a lot of Dollard's arguments have a somewhat familiar ring, perhaps reflecting the influence of George Herbert Mead. He notes that 'as soon as we take the post of observer on the cultural level the individual is lost in the crowd and our concepts never lead us back to him. After we have 'gone cultural' we experience the person as a fragment of a (derived) culture pattern, as a marionette dancing on the strings of (reified) culture forms' (p.5). In contrast to this the Life Historian;

> Can see his life history subject as a link in a chain of social transmission. There were links before him from which he acquired his present culture. Other links will follow him to which he will pass on the current of tradition.

The life history attempts to describe a unit in that process: it is a study of one of the strands of a complicated collective life which has historical continuity (p.15).

Dollard is especially good, though perhaps unfashionably polemical, in his discussion of the tension between what might be called the 'cultural legacy', the weight of collective tradition and expectation, and the individual's unique history and capacity for interpretation and action. By focussing on this tension, Dollard argues, the life history offers ethnographers a way of exploring between the culture, the social structure and individual lives. Thus Dollard believed that in the best life history work 'we must constantly keep in mind the situation both as defined by others and by the subject, such a history will not only define both versions but let us see clearly the pressure of the formal situation and the force of the inner private definition of the situation' (p.32). This resolution, or attempt to address a common tension, is seen as valuable because 'whenever we encounter difference between our official or average or cultural expectation of action in a 'situation' and the actual conduct of the person this indicates the presence of a private interpretation' (p. 32).

After reaching its peak in the 1930's the life history approach fell from grace and was largely abandoned by social scientists. This was firstly because the increasingly powerful advocacy of statistical methods gained a growing number of adherents among sociologists, but perhaps also because among ethnographically-inclined sociologists more emphasis came to be placed on situation rather than on biography as the basis for understanding human behaviour.

Since the 1930's little attention has been paid by mainstream sociologists to life history methods. Only recently have there been signs of rehabilitation, significantly among deviancy sociologists: studies of a transsexual (Bogdan, 1974), a professional fence (Klockars, 1975) and, with a fine sense of history, once again a professional thief (Chambliss, 1972). Other marginal groups re-exploring life history methods are journalists-cum-sociologists, like Studs Terkel (1975) in the USA and Jeremy Seabrook (1976) and Ronald Blythe (1969) in the UK, and a growing band of so-called 'Oral Historians' (Thompson, 1978).

Among these scholars, albeit in marginal or fragmented groups, a debate is underway which promises a thoroughgoing re-examination of the potential of life history methods. See especially the works of M. Huberman, (1993), P. Munro (1998), K. Plummer (2001). But before we consider the contemporary appeal of the life history and apply this to ethnographic studies of the school, it is important to discover why life history method was for so long eclipsed by the social survey and by participant observation. In this examination the emphasis will be on distinguishing fundamental methodological stumbling blocks from the political and personal reasons for the decline of life history work.

REASONS FOR THE DECLINE OF THE LIFE HISTORY

By 1966 Becker was able to summarise the fate of the life history method among American sociologists in this manner: 'given the variety of scientific uses to which the life history may be put, one must wonder at the relative neglect into which it has fallen' (Becker, 1970). Becker notes that sociologists have never given up life histories altogether but neither have they made it one of their standard research tools. The general pattern was, and is, that: they know of life history studies 'and assign them for their students to read. But they do not ordinarily think of gathering life history documents or of making the technique part of their research approach' (pp.71-2).

The reasons for the decline of life history methods are partly specific to the Chicago department. From the late 1920's life histories came under increasing fire as the debate within the department between the virtues of case study (and life histories) and statistical techniques intensified. Faris in his study of Chicago sociology records a landmark within this debate:

> To test this issue, Stouffer had hundreds of students write autobiographies instructing them to include everything in their life experiences relating to alcohol usage and the prohibition law. Each of these autobiographies was read by a panel of persons presumed to be qualified in life history research, and for each subject the reader indicated on a scaled line the position of the subject's attitude regarding prohibition. Inter-reader agreement was found to be satisfactory.

> Each of the same subjects had also filled out a questionnaire that formed a scale of the Thurstone type. The close agreement of the scale measurement of each subject's attitude with the reader's estimate of the life history indicated that, as far as the scale score was concerned, nothing was gained by the far more lengthy and laborious process of writing and judging a life history' (Faris, 1967, pp.114-5).

Even within Chicago case study work the life history declined as against other ethnographic devices, notably participant observation. One element of the explanation of this lies perhaps in the orientations of Blumer and Hughes. These two sociologists provide a bridge between the Chicago school of the 1920's and 1930's and those Matza has termed the 'neoChicagoans' such as Becker and Goffman. Blumer's symbolic interactionism places primary emphasis on process and situation, and explanations in terms of biography like those in terms of social structural forces, are regarded with considerable suspicion. Hughes' comparative approach to the study of occupations may have tended to limit interest in biography in favour of a concern with the typical problems faced by occupational practitioners and the strategies they adopt for dealing with them. An additional factor, which hastened the decline of the methodological eclecticism of Chicago sociology with the life history playing a central role, was the decline of Chicago itself as a dominant centre for sociological studies.

The fate of life history methods is inextricably linked to the evolving aspirations of sociology as a discipline. Hence the methodological weaknesses of the life history method came to be set against the need to develop abstract theory. When sociology was highly concerned with providing detailed accounts of specific communities, institutions or organisations such weaknesses were clearly of less account. But in the life history of sociology the pervasive drift of academic disciplines towards abstract theory has been irresistibly followed: in this evolutionary imperative it is not difficult to discern the desire of sociologists to gain parity of esteem with other academic disciplines. The resulting pattern of mainstream sociology meant that sociologists came to pursue 'data formulated in the abstract categories of their own theories rather than in the categories that seemed most relevant to the people they studied' (Becker, 1970, p. 72).

Alongside the move towards abstract academic theory sociological method became more 'professional'. Essentially this led towards a model of *single study* research defined by Becker in this way:

I use the term to refer to research projects that are conceived of as self-sufficient and self-contained, which provide all the evidence one needs to accept or reject the conclusions they proffer...The single study is integrated with the main body of knowledge in the following way: it derives its hypotheses from an inspection of what is already known; then, after the research is completed, if those hypotheses have been demonstrated, they are added to the wall of what is already scientifically known and used as the basis for further studies. The important point is that the researcher's hypothesis is either proved or disproved on the basis of what he has discovered in doing that one piece of research' (Becker, 1970, p. 72).

The imperative towards this pattern of sociological research can be clearly evidenced in the traditions and organisational format of emergent professional sociology. The PhD student must define and test *his* hypothesis; the journal article must test the author's own or other academics' hypotheses; the research project or programme must state the generalisable aims and locate the burden of what has to be proved. But this dominant experimental model, so fruitful in analogies with other *sciences,* and hence so crucial in legitimating sociology as a fully-fledged academic discipline, led to the neglect of sociology's full range of methodology and data sources.

It has led people to ignore the other functions of research and particularly to ignore the contribution made by one study to an overall research enterprise even when the study, considered in isolation, produced no definitive results of its own. Since, by these criteria, the life history did not produce definite results, people have been at a loss to make anything of it and by and large have declined to invest the time and effort necessary to acquire life history documents (Becker, 1970 p.73).

Becker ends by holding out the hope that sociologists will in the future develop a 'further understanding of the complexity of the scientific enterprise', that this will rehabilitate the life history method and lead to a new range of life history documents as generative as those produced by the Chicago sociologists in the 1920's and 1930's.

In the period following Becker's strictures, sociology has been subject to a number of new directions which have sought to re-embrace some of the elements lost in the 'positivist', theory-testing models (Morris, 1977; Cuff and Payne, 1979). However, the one new direction which clearly stresses biography, the phenomenological sociology of Berger and Luckmann (see Berger, 1963, and Berger and Luckmann, 1967), has led to little empirical work as yet. Hence research in interpretive sociology has displayed a heavy emphasis on situation, under the influence of interactionism and ethno-methodology. The paradox is that the new directions in sociology have moved away from the 'positivist' model, but directly to situation and occasion, and as a result life history and biography have *remained* at the sidelines of the sociological enterprise. For instance, interactionist studies have focussed on the perspectives and definitions emerging among groups of actors in particular situations, the backcloth to this being presented as a somewhat monolithic 'structural' or 'cultural legacy' which constrains, in a rather disconnected manner, the actors' potentialities. In over-reacting to more deterministic models, this situational emphasis most commonly fails to make any connection with historical process. Thus, while interactionists retained their interest in the meaning objects had for actors, these meanings increasingly came to be seen as collectively generated to deal with specific situations, rather than as the product of individual or even collective biography.

Viewing sociology's evolution over half a century or so provides a number of insights into the life history method. Firstly, as sociologists began to take seriously their social scientific pursuit of generalisable facts and the development of abstract theory, life history work came to be seen as having serious methodological flaws. In addition, since life history studies often appeared to be only 'telling tales' these methodological reservations were enhanced by the generally low status of this as an 'academic' or 'scientific' exercise. Paradoxically even when antidotes to the experimental model of sociology developed these took the form of interactionism and ethno-methodology both of which stressed situation and occasion rather than biography and background. Moreover, since these new directions had status problems of their own, life history work was unattractive on this count as well. At the conference where the present paper was originally delivered, a classroom interactionist rejected the exhortation to consider life history work by saying:- 'We should not suggest new methodologies of this sort…because of the problems of our academic careers. Christ! Ethnography is low status enough as it is'. Set against the life history of the aspirant academic we clearly see the unattractiveness of the life history method.

Leaving aside the political and personal reservations over life histories however, there are clearly important methodological problems. Two major problems underpin the opposition of sociologists to the method. Firstly there is the problem of *representativeness* or *typicality*. The aspiration to develop generalisable insights has intrinsic as well as political justifications. Life history work cannot guarantee typicality, representativeness or, therefore, contributions to general theory. At the same time there is a second problem that life histories are a considerable undertaking. With low guarantees of generalizable findings, then, they couple the awkward necessity for *large time commitments.*

REHABILITATING LIFE HISTORY: PROBLEMS AND POSSIBILITIES

To rehabilitate the life history we need to indicate its relationship to sociological theory and alongside this to overcome the other major objection, the time-consuming nature of the exercise.

As we noted earlier some deviancy sociologists have recently embraced life history methods and are engaged in trying to resolve the ambivalence between the method and sociological theory. Faraday and Plummer (1979) present the relationship of life history to their theoretical enterprise in three ways: in the *examination* of existing theory (as Becker, 1970 p.67 says "even though the life history does not in itself provide definitive proof of a proposition it can be a negative case that forces us to decide a proposed theory is inadequate"); in the *exploration* of data 'in order to generate sensitising concepts, theories and conceptual frameworks'. In areas of enquiry in which little is known the life history therefore provides 'a sensitising tool to the kinds of issue and problems involved in the field'. Finally life history *utilises* theory.

> There is no intrinsic disconnection of the life history from theoretical work. It is clearly not very good at testing or validating existing theory, although it might be useful in finding a falsificatory case. It is quiet good when combined with a general orientation in theory which enables one to see how the theory might make sense of that field as a whole, but in no conclusive way. It is at its best when it is being used in an exploratory fashion for generating many concepts, hunches and ideas, both at the local and situational level and on a historical structural level and within the same field and in *relationship* to other fields' (Faraday and Plummer, 1979, pp. 773-795).

In general the life history is congruent with the main theoretical assumption of interactionism that the individual life is not as clear or ordered as many social science accounts, especially those following the experimental model, would have us believe. The greatest strength of the life history is in its penetration of the subjective reality of the individual: it allows the subject to 'speak for herself or himself'. But above and beyond this, the life history 'can give meaning to the overworked notion of *process'* (Becker, 1970, p.69). In the experimental model we might give people a questionnaire at various stages in their life and attribute a process to the changing answers at different periods. But there is a gap in such a procedure: the life history can fill that gap. The well-documented life history:

> Will give us the details of that process whose character we would otherwise only be able to speculate about, and the process to which our data must

ultimately be referred if they are to have theoretical and not just an operational and predictive significance. It will describe those crucial interactive episodes in which new lines of individual and collective activity are forged, in which new aspects of the self are brought into being. It is by thus giving a realistic basis to our imagery of the underlying process that the life history serves the purposes of checking assumptions, illuminating organisation and re-orienting stagnant fields (Becker, 1970, p. 70).

The focus of the life history is clear: the personal 'reality' and process. The life historian is initially only concerned with grasping personal truth: 'on the (more important) issue of attaining universal truth he or she remains mute'. The problem of this focus, as with much of interactionism, is that the personal experience and process often gets divorced from the wider socio-historical structure. The life historian must constantly broaden the concern with personal truth to take account of wider socio-historical concerns *even if these are not part of the consciousness of the individual.* The fully researched life history should then allow us.

To see an individual in relation to the history of his time, and how he is influenced by the various religious, social, psychological and economic currents present in his world. It permits us to view the intersection of the life history of men with the history of society, thereby enabling us to understand better the choices, contingencies and options open to the individual' (Bogdan, 1974, p. 4).

In rehabilitating the life history it is important to see the sociological enterprise not as monolithic but as multi-faceted. Becker's image of the mosaic is useful: 'each piece added to a mosaic adds a little to our understanding' or Levi-Strauss's analogy with the jigsaw. Seen in this way the place of life histories should become evident. The object is not to resolve the tension between experimental and interactionist models: both have a place. The questionnaire can test pre-selected themes but in doing so closes off avenues of exploration; in complement, interactionist studies and life histories trace the personal situation and life in evolution. By rehabilitating the life history the jigsaw puzzle might finally fall into place, for there is always a better chance if all the pieces are used.

LIFE HISTORY AND THE STUDY OF SCHOOLING

The Contemporary Situation: A Brief Review

In reviewing the history of sociology, it has been argued that the experimental model of sociological investigation, with its emphasis on single studies to test pre-selected hypotheses, whilst for long dominant, has neglected participant perspectives and interactional processes. Paradoxically the interactionist and ethno-methodological models, which have sought to explore these neglected areas, have focussed on situation and occasion with the result that biography and historical background have continued to be neglected. To a great extent these patterns of development for sociology in general hold true when one reviews the sociology of schooling.

Reviewing contemporary interactionist and ethno-methodological studies of schooling one might discern two characteristic assumptions. Firstly because of the focus on situation and occasion, little attention has been given to the individual biography, personal views and life-style of teachers. Partly this may have arisen by anthropological analogy. For instance, Philip Jackson's work on *Life in Classrooms,* although full of insight, presents teachers as a particular kind of species reproducing within busy, tiring and unchanging environments:

> Not only is the classroom a relatively stable physical environment, it also provides a fairly constant social context. Behind the same old desks sit the same old students, in front of the familiar blackboard stands the familiar teacher (Jackson, 1968, p. 166).

As a result in these accounts the teacher becomes depersonalised, neutral above all eminently *interchangeable:* the same old familiar teacher we know so well.

A second characteristic assumption is also epitomised in Jackson, the assumption of *timelessness:* this is at one with interchangeability – whatever the time, whoever the teacher, everything is much the same. This anti-historical approach is also a feature of interactionist and especially ethno methodological approaches:

> a fundamental assumption of the ethno-methodological approach is that the social world is essentially an ongoing achieved world. The everyday world of social events, settings and relationships is all the time created and achieved by the members of society and these events, settings and relationships are assumed to have no existence independent of the occasion of their production (Payne, 1976, p.33).

But while there is some truth in this, the actors creating the social events which Payne describes do nevertheless have an existence which is independent of, and previous to, the social events in which they are involved. Such a neglect of historical and biographical background makes problematic the construction of general categories within which to situate these ethno-methodological and interactionist accounts of specific events. Hence, it would be possible for a variety of social events to be portrayed, and for their internal logic to be laid bare, without getting at any general understanding of why events differ and why what is common to certain events, in this case school lessons, recurs over time. A knowledge of personal biographies and historical background would add breadth and depth to the studies and fulfil the aspiration, indeed obligation, to develop more generalisable categories of understanding.

Two characteristic assumptions in ethno-methodology and interactionism have been discerned: those of teacher *interchangeability* and of *timelessness.* As noted, these new approaches have shared with the dominant 'positivist' model of sociology a neglect of personal biography and historical background. The existence of these two characteristic assumptions will not be proven at length in this chapter.

The study of a book like *School Experience* (Woods and Hammersley, 1977) would however confirm that there are grounds for believing that these characteristic assumptions are common and influential in the direction and selection of studies of schooling by ethno-methodologists and interactionists. Similarly, that excellent study *Deviance in Classrooms* (Hargreaves, Hester and Mellor, 1975), although marked by an eclecticism of approach, nonetheless misses many opportunities to follow up biographical data. The authors concede that teachers often 'import' life history data into accounts of their practice but as is so often the case, this data is edited out in the final version. Even the most recent work displays this tendency with its focus on generalised teacher and pupil strategies (Woods, 1980a and 1980b). Yet elsewhere Woods (1979, p.3) has noted that 'the social scientist has to begin to develop a perspective that enables him to develop the connection between macro-sociological and historical processes on the one hand and individual biographies on the other'. But in the absence of life history data this can only remain a pious hope. We are left in the position of having a clearly discerned portrait and analysis of a series of differentiated teacher strategies, without any understanding of how particular teachers come to adopt particular strategies. In understanding something so intensely personal as teaching it is critical that we know about the person the teacher is: our paucity of knowledge in this area is a manifest indictment of the range of our sociological imagination.

Broadening the qualitative approach

To avoid wandering too far in criticising qualitative approaches there is the need to once again reaffirm the commitment to such approaches: many of the arguments in the introductory pages have after all been used in the past to support participant observation. Denzin (1970, p.70) has summarised the position rather well: 'The life history parallels participant observation. Its basic difference lies in the breadth of coverage, not in causal intent'.

We have argued that interactionist and ethno-methodological studies of schooling have generated a predominant but implausible model of the teacher: largely interchangeable, subject to timeless problems and employing a variety of standard but apparently spontaneously developed strategies to deal with them. Whilst not wishing to argue that teachers do not have important characteristics in common we argue that there are important distinctions in attitudes, performance and strategies which can be identified in different teachers and at different times. To understand the degree of importance of these distinctions we have to reconnect our studies of schooling with investigations of personal biography and historical background: above all we are arguing for a reintegration of situational with biographical and historical analyses. Through such a reintegration we might move away from studies where the human actor is studied in a manner contrivedly divorced from his own biography and history of the situation. A model of human action is required which points to the role of both situational and biographical/historical factors and their interrelation.

Programmatic arguments for new directions are however relatively easy. The rest of the article tentatively defines the major dimensions of life history investigation and then seeks to illustrate this through two examples of recent work in the field. Essentially, my argument involves four claims placed below in order of ascending generality (and, possibly, difficulty):

— that the teacher's *previous career and life experience* shape his view of teaching and the way he sets about it;

— that the teacher's *life outside school,* his *latent identities and cultures,* may have an important impact on his work as a teacher. This relates to 'central life interests' and commitments (as in the case of a teacher recently interviewed who burst out 'but you must understand that my whole centre of gravity is elsewhere, well outside these bloody school walls'). Becker and Geer's (1971) (p.56-60) work provides a theoretical basis here;

— that the teacher's *career* is a vitally important research focus. Bogdan and Taylor (1970, p.121) have argued that in the life history 'the researcher codes the subject's words according to certain phases or periods in his or her life, what many qualitative researchers call a previous *career'.* The work of Strauss, Hughes and Becker, provides a conceptual base (Becker et al, 1961). Also notable is Becker's study of *'The Career of the Chicago Public School Teacher',* which is premised on the belief that the concept of career is 'of great use in understanding the dynamics of work organisations and the movement and fate of individuals within them' (Becker, 1952, p.470).

— that we must, following Bogdan, seek to locate the life history of the individual within 'the history of his time'. Clearly there are limits to this aspiration with regard to schooling. But 'life histories' of schools, subjects, and the teaching profession would provide vital contextual information. For instance if we compare below the school Kensington in its early years with the situation after 1979 it is almost as if the teacher would be encountering different micro-worlds altogether, the same could be said in comparing the innovative Leicestershire school Countersthorpe in its early years around 1970 with it's subsequent restructuring in the years after 1980: it is surely not possible to regard such changes in 'arena' as variables to be held constant in the study of teachers in action.

In adding this fourth investigative focus we are, Bogdan notwithstanding, broadening the traditional domain of life history to include the 'life histories' of collectivities. Life historians have however noted the need to locate the individual life experience 'within the broader socio-historical framework'. In studies of schooling this is particularly important and for this reason I have chosen examples of life history work which take this focus.

The two studies which are described in the next section have been chosen to illustrate how profitable life histories might be and to show that quite wide-ranging biographical and historical studies can be completed with a reasonable economy of time. Both examples attempt to link the life histories of key participants within the life histories of collectivities, in one case a school, in the other a school subject. (In both cases all that can be presented in such a short article are short summaries of the research: to do these studies justice the reader is recommended to consult the original work).

'Kensington Revisited'

Louis Smith's work in the ethnography of schooling spans the last twenty-five years. In the *Complexities of an Urban Classroom* (Smith and Geoffrey, 1968), he studied the classroom teacher in action and later in 1971 in *The Anatomy of Educational Innovation* (Smith and Keith, 1971) he produced a detailed organisational analysis of one showpiece elementary school innovation, being concerned with the dynamics of educational change at work in a particular school at a specific point in time.

He has come to view this work as limited in a number of ways and has set out to remedy these limitations. This new research on the same educational institution, Kensington School, attempts to answer two questions: Firstly what is the current structure of Kensington as an educational organisation and has the school reverted to its pre-innovational pattern? Secondly, what interpretation/explanation can be made of the changes that have occurred between 1964 and 1979? Smith notes in his research proposal that 'Methodologically this will involve a special kind of case study, a mix of ethnography and recent history'. Participant observation, interviews/oral history, and primary documents e.g. local newspapers, school records and bulletins are viewed as sources of data.

Central to Smith's research follow-up are these two questions: 'what has happened to the original staff?' and 'How do they perceive the impact of the Kensington experience on their professional lives?' He writes:

> In answering these questions the hope would be to capture each part of the school and its original faculty at a second period in time, to make comparisons and to draw inferences about innovation and its effects on the lives of a small group of people'.

Smith asserts that the major concern here is 'to place the issues of educational innovation into the broader context of the individual's *life*' (Smith, 1980).

A good deal of the research pursuing these issues deals with the individual headmasters of Kensington. Data on these key individuals was often collected by retrospective interviews with members of staff at Kensington. The impact of the different perspectives of the first headmaster, Eugene Shelby, and the second, Michael Edwards, are eloquently caught in a series of such interviews as evidenced in the following transcript:

Teacher: The kids were not allowed to make as many choices. (In Shelby's era) they were allowed to make choices all day long. And choices in important things such as 'Do I want to go to math class today, or do I want to go out and play?' And if they wanted to go out and play, they played. The first year I was there and we divided up for classes, there were three of us, and the first morning when we changed (students) 'You go here for this class, here for that class', half of our group went out the door. I said, 'Where are you going?' I ran after them. 'We're going for fishing poles'. I said, 'No you're not. What do you want fishing poles for?' 'Oh, we're going down to the creek to fish'. And they all came back in and we started to ask questions.

Observer: So was that tightened up then?

Teacher: Oh yeah, right away. We simply did that. 'You may go out at recess time and we'll do that, but you don't have that choice now. We will go to maths class when it's time. We will go to social studies class when its time.'

Observer: Now was that Mr. Edwards' influence, or the teachers' influence?

Teacher: Right at that point it was a teachers'. We went to him and said, 'This is what happened, and this is what we did at the moment'. And I can remember the three of us talking to him about it, and he said, 'Oh no, the kids *will* have class'...Once we said to the kids, 'This is the way we're going to do it now, we're all new and this is what we've decided to do'. There was nothing else, we did it that way. And the amazing part of this, the kids never said...or very seldom said, 'But last year we...'I always found that very amazing.

Observer: So they adjusted and adapted quite easily.

Teacher: Yeah, and another thing I remember is when I passed out textbooks, the kids were terribly excited, 'This is my book?' 'Yes, it's your book' 'All year'. They really liked that textbook that they could keep in their desk. (Smith, L. et al, 1985, pp. 18-19)

The initial focus has moved however from a concern with individual teachers life histories to a more broadly concerned pattern of investigation of the life history of an elementary school. The mode of investigation is now dignified as a 'longitudinal nested systems model'. Smith in his most recent, and as yet provisional paper, describes the genesis of the model in this way.

We have moved from an initial set of predictions and the beginnings of a new perspective into a lengthy discussion of Kensington's history. When we sought to explain the changes in the School, we found ourselves drawn into two dimensions or contexts, time and space. Kensington School's immediate geographical and social context is the Milford School District. It was not surprising to find both the School and the District to have interdependent histories. As we began exploring these histories we found plots and themes that enmeshed with even more far ranging contexts. It was as if Kensington's history was circumscribed by Milford's, and these two in increasingly broader contexts in space and time. When we first conceived of returning to Kensington School, its fifteen year history seemed to define our task. We found that we could not explain the changes in this once innovative school with such a narrow conception. Our search for antecedents has pushed us back near the turn of the Century and widened our view to include Suburban County, Midwest State, the United States, and even the world community. The changes we found at Kensington originate in the histories of each of these broader systems. Our notion of 'Longitudinal Nested Systems' is an effort to come to grips with the role of these interdependent systems in shaping the school we found on our return visit (Smith, L. et al, pp.18-19).

The 'search for antecedents' is clearly open-ended and in such a brief description the focus might appear far too broad. In fact the study does not move far away from a detailed concern with explaining the changes at Kensington School and the broad spectrum of potential antecedents are closely defined and related to the school in question. The chart (on page 146) notes the levels of investigation (Smith, L et al, pp. 18-19).

The first section of the history of the Kensington innovation is told through the periods of each headmaster's incumbency: Shelbys brief 'Innovative Lighthouse' 1964-66, 'The Revisionary Decade' of Michael Edwards (first section the 'golden era' 1966-72), 'Marking Time' the Hawkins era 1976-79, and the 'current period of traditional stabilization' John Wales 1979 onwards. Each era is viewed through life history data on the headmasters and personal testimony from the staff. The school superintendents of Milford School District are similarly treated within the context of a history of this district since 1910.

By broadening the focus of historical investigation from headmasters' life histories to life histories, to life histories of the school and the school district, the whole manner of study can be transformed. Smith concludes that he was:

> Trying for a description and analysis of changes in the innovative Kensington School between its opening in 1964 and its current status fifteen years later in 1979-80. As a piece of contemporary empirical social science research that represents a long time period. From an historical point of view it is not only recent history but also a relatively short time period. One aspect of our meta-theoretical perspective assumes that a view of the history of the Milford School District will enhance our understanding of the changes in the Kensington School. More recently, as our data has accumulated, as new directions for inquiry have arisen out of available people, documents, and themes and as analysis and interpretations have continued, we have found shifts in the very nature of the problem. Now one of our guiding questions is not so much 'How and why did this school change from 1964 to 1979?' but also 'Why did the Kensington School appear at all in the Milford School District?' Such is the process of inquiry (Smith, L., et al, pp.18-19).

Essentially this historical study allows us to move to a view of 'innovation as aberration' – a perspective some way from Smith's 1971 study.

Smith's work therefore moves from an initial concern to study the impact of innovation on teachers and headmasters' lives to an attempt to locate these within the history of the district and the times. The momentum of this ascending order of study is somewhat breathless in the present account because of the need to compress our summary of is research. But if Smith's work serves best to illustrate the methodological dynamic at work in the pursuit of life history study the second instance illustrates in rather more detail the kind of material which is actually generated in life history interviews.

'SCHOOL SUBJECTS AND CURRICULUM CHANGE'

The aim of the study reported in *School Subjects and Curriculum Change* (Goodson, 1982) was to trace the reasons behind the promotion of a new school subject: Environmental Studies. The research method employed was to begin by collecting the life histories of the major participants in the promotion of this new subject. The patterns of decision, the changes of direction and the stated rationales given by these promoters of the subject were echoed in the evolutionary profile of the subject, which was later reconstructed. In a real sense the life histories of these key personnel constituted the life history of the subject in question.

The main advocate of the subject began his teaching in a secondary modern school. His career after leaving school was interrupted by the war and, having undergone 'emergency training' after the war in rural studies, this teacher had a vision of his subject as the 'curriculum link' connecting school to environment and life.

> I had a strong feeling that education wasn't just book learning, it involved common sense applied to a problem – I talked to many farmers and they would talk about the kind of intelligence a farm worker would need to apply to his job. (Interview with Sean Carson, April 8th 1976).

Moreover the 'best boys, the most able, who today would be in the sixth form went into farming gladly' so that in the beginning his subject was not restricted to the least able students who attended the Secondary Modern Schools.

As the tripartite system of education gradually emerged in the form of new school buildings and modified curricula, it became clear that rural studies was only developing in secondary modern schools. Furthermore secondary modern schools were increasingly concerning themselves with external examinations. His classes began to change their composition:

> The advent of external examinations gradually prevented the more capable children from taking part and eventually led the scheme to be aimed at the less able children only.

In moving to teach in Hertfordshire the changing pattern became still more evident. The adviser in the county had been a leading advocate of rural studies as the 'hub of the curriculum' integrating school and environment but the head of the new school 'didn't see rural education I that sense':

> He was already thinking ahead to raising the standards of this school to what would eventually be C.S.E. None of this existed, but he was thinking in term of this. Although I understood when I got here that I could have anyone who wanted to volunteer for my subject it never in fact worked out. The classes were streamed. I only ever got the lower of the three streams.

A further problem followed:

> While at first I could do what I liked with that bottom stream and I did the same sort of thing as in Kent, over the next few years this was whittled away from me as more specialism invaded the curriculum, and these kids eventually spent practically no time running the farm.

The result of the 'whittling away' of rural studies as more specialism invaded the curriculum was that the more examination-oriented subjects began to take most of the financial resources. Rural studies had a standard of provision below even the other practical subjects (which were themselves badly under-resourced). The subject 'had to adapt or perish'.

> By now I saw rural studies as a specialist subject with weak links. My alternative vision was that it could have been an all pervasive educational approach...

> ...By 1954 I'd already given up hope of getting rural studies seen in the way I'd taught it in Kent...That's the sort of dreams I was well aware of giving up...a lot of kids don't learn through paper and pencil...we do far too much of this. A lot of kids could achieve success and use all the skills that we talk about in the classroom, such as analysing and comparing, through physical activities...With the farm it was a completely renewing set of problems and the fact that it was a farm was incidental. (Interview with Sean Carson, April 8th 1976).

In retrospect the renunciation of this vision of rural studies has come to be viewed as the crucial turning point in trying to develop a subject of interest to most pupils. The promotion of the subject to win resources meant that these pupil needs had to be foregone: 'I've always felt dissatisfied since. I've met many teachers who'd come across the same realisation. (Interview with Sean Carson, April 8th 1976)

But at the same time the promotion of the subject was seen as the most important consideration particularly as in 1958 he had become as Adviser in Rural Education. His visits to schools convinced him of the need for more resources and he saw enhanced status as the strategy for demanding more resources. In particular he called a meeting of County Rural Studies Associations with a view to forming a National Association. He saw this as 'a way to raise the standard and status of rural studies because we decided that unless it was raised nationally we wouldn't be able to do it in my county'.

However, the Association made little headway in gaining status for the subject. By 1962 'it became increasingly obvious to me and one or two others, that it wasn't going to get anywhere!' The reason was that resources and status were invested in examination subjects. The problem for rural studies was that as a practical subject it was hardly amenable to written examinations. As examinations in the subject were tested one teacher protested that: 'Once again we see the unwanted children of lower intelligence being made servants of the juggernaut of documented evidence, the inflated examination' (P.L Quant, Journal of Rural Studies, March 1967, page 6).

These protests had to be overcome if status and resources were to be won.

I.G.　　　　Why did you finally 'embrace' examinations?

The Adviser: Because if you didn't, you wouldn't get any money, any status, any intelligent kids.

I.G.　　　　Did you ever think 'this is going to be a big problem...'?

The Adviser: No, I didn't se that as clearly as I maybe should have done. I just thought 'If you're outside this you've had it in schools'. It was already happening in some schools. Where a rural studies teacher was leaving they didn't fill the place, because they gave it to someone in the examination set.

I.G.　　　　So you had to climb aboard?

The Adviser: Yes, or rural studies would have definitely disappeared.

In promoting rural studies as an examination subject a new problem arose. The subject had always been taught in secondary moderns, normally to the least able. 'We therefore felt that we were labouring under a heading of Rural Studies which had certain connotations in the eyes of many people and that really the word rural wasn't right.'

As a result a changeover to Environmental Studies was promoted. An 'A' level scheme based in the county where he served as an adviser was planned:

We decided that the only way to make progress was to get in on the examination racket...we must draw up an examination...we decided that the exam was essential because otherwise you couldn't be equal with any other subject. Another thing was that comprehensive education was coming in: once that came in, no teacher who didn't teach in the fifth or sixth form was going to count for two pence. So you had to have an 'A' level for teachers to aim at.

In 1973 five years before his (premature) retirement an 'A' level in Environmental Studies was accepted by the Schools Council. However, the battle for acceptance was fiercely contested, causing bouts of ill-health and exhaustion, and in the end the range of limitations put on the new 'A' level were such as to threaten its viability. Environmental Studies has not proved the vehicle for status that it was conceived as and upon his retirement his replacement was in the field of multi-cultural education and world studies.

I have dealt at some length with one life history episode covering the years 1945-78, the active professional years in the career of one influential teacher and adviser. I have done so in order to show how life history data can provide insights into the changing stages in a teacher's view of his work. This evolution has to be set against the changing patterns of educational organisation and examination systems, more particularly the specific context of the school subject has also to be presented in evolution: in this example the symbiosis of individual life history and subject history is unusually strong but it is nonetheless symptomatic.

The teacher's career pattern in this instance reflects a move away from practically-oriented pedagogy towards high-status academic pedagogy directed towards formal written examinations. The reasons for the transition in this teacher's life history are clearly instanced but they help elucidating a process that is familiar and fundamental in recent English educational history. By focussing on the individual tensions and dissatisfactions in the process of educational 'progress' new insights are developed. The teacher, who later becomes an adviser, is seen in the process of compromise between pedagogic ideals and professional status enhancement: moving from an 'idealistic' phase in the thirties towards frustration and uncertainty in the forties and finally career and subject aggrandisement in the fifties.

The implications of the life history for teachers' classroom ideologies' have recently been tentatively examined by Scheinfeld and Messerschmidt. Their study looks at teachers of different ages, one of 25 and another of 34. The differences in their teaching styles are related to their different life stages, most notable are the different centres of gravity. The younger teacher 'exhausts herself in teaching' and 'alludes to a limited life beyond her work in the classroom'. The older teacher 'has accepted teaching as her vocation' but 'vocation is not the only concern; there is a life beyond work'. 'She does not confront the occupational structure (like the younger teacher), but rather the world outside the occupational structure' (Scheinfeld and Messerschmidt, 1978, Mimeo).

Whilst these insights are fairly commonsensical what is new is Scheinfeld and Messerschmidt's systematic attempt to relate the teachers' life-stages to classroom pedagogy. The study of the genesis of Environmental Studies also confirms an evolutionary link between subjects, subject pedagogy and personal life stages. It is surely time these links were explored and that classroom events were investigated within the context of teachers' life histories, and the histories of the subjects they teach, the profession to which they belong, and the schools in which they teach.

CONCLUSION

This chapter has argued that studies of schooling have neglected personal and collective biographies and that to remedy this deficiency life history data should be collected. We have noted that even interactionist and ethno-methodological work has neglected biography, by concentrating on the occasion or the event, most notably the school lesson. These studies have been characterized by assumptions of timelessness and teacher inter-changeability. To remedy these failings the life history must be rehabilitated, we must explore elements of individual difference and change through personal biography, and integrate these with historical factors by studying the evolving background of the teachers' professional lives. The latter emphasis leads us to view the individual against the broader patterns of evolution in schooling: such as the development of school innovations, school subjects, educational systems and the teaching profession itself.

In life history work, then, we gain insights into the way in which, over time, individuals come to terms with the constraints and conditions in which they work, and how these relate to the wider social structure. As a result, the fate envisaged by Hargreaves (1978, p.9) of ethnography deteriorating 'into a proliferation of unique case studies' should be avoided. The life history approach has the potential to make a far-reaching contribution to the perennial problem of understanding the links between 'personal troubles' and 'public issues', a task which, as C. Wright Mills (1959) pointed out many years ago, is the essence of the sociological enterprise.

ACKNOWLEDGEMENTS

To *Interchange* (Ontario) for publishing an earlier and much shorter version of this paper in their *March 1981* Volume

REFERENCES

Allport, G. (1942). *The use of personal documents in psychological science*. New York: SSRC.
Anderson, N. (1923). *The hobo*. University of Chicago Press.
Becker, H. S. (1952). The career of the Chicago public school teacher. *American Journal of Sociology, 57*.
Becker, H. S., et al. (1961). *Boys in white*. University of Chicago Press.
Becker, H. S. (1970). *Sociological work: Method and substance*. Chicago: Aldine.
Becker, H. S., & Geer, B. (1971). Latent culture: A note on the theory of latent social roles. In B. R. Cosin, et al. (Ed.), *School and society: A sociological reader*. London: RKP.
Berger, P. (1963). *Invitation to sociology*. Doubleday.
Berger, P., & Luckmann, T. (1967). *The social construction of reality*. Allen Lane.
Bertaux, D. (1981). *Biography and society: The life history approach in the social sciences*. Sage.
Blythe, R. (1969). *Akenfield*. Allen Lane.
Bogdan, R. (1974). *Being different: The autobiography of Jane Fry*. Wiley.
Bogdan, R., & Taylor, S. (1970). *Introduction to qualitative research methods*. Wiley.
Chambliss, W. (1972). *Boxman: A professional thief's journey*. Harper & Row.
Conwell, C., & Sutherland, E. (1937). *The professional thief*. Chicago.
Cuff, E., & Payne, G. (1979). *Sociological Methods: A sourcebook*. London: Butterworths.
Denzin, N. (1970). *Sociological methods: A sourcebook*. London: Butterworths.
Dollard, J. (1949). *Criteria for the life history*. Yale University Press.
Faraday, A., & Plummer, K. (1979). Doing life histories. *Sociological Review, 27*(4).
Faris, R. (1967). *Chicago sociology*. University of Chicago Press.
Goodson, I. F. (1982). *Schools subjects and curriculum change*. London: Croom Helm.
Hargreaves, D. (1978). Whatever happened to symbolic interactionism? In L. Barton & R. Meighan (Eds.), *Sociological interpretations of schooling and classrooms: A reappraisal*. Nafferton Books.
Hargreaves, D., Hester, S., & Mellor, F. (1975). *Deviance in classrooms*. RKP.
Huberman, M. (1993). *The lives of teachers*. New York Teachers College Press.
Interview with Sean Carson. (1976, April 8).
Jackson, P. W. (1968). *Life in classrooms*. New York: Rinehart and Winston.
Klockars, C. (1975). *The professional fence*. Tavistock.
Morris, M. (1977). *An excursion into creative sociology*. Blackwell.
Munro, P. (1998). *Subject to fiction: Women teachers' life history narratives and the cultural politics of resistance*. Philadelphia: Open University Press.
Plummer, K. (2001). *Documents of life 2: An invitation to critical humanism*. Fowles and Oakes, CA: Sage.
Payne, G. (1976). Making a lesson happen. In M. Hammersley & P. Woods (Eds.), *Schooling and society: A reader*. Open University.

Quant, P. L. (1967, March). *Journal* of *Rural Studies*.

Scheinfield, D., & Messerschmidt, D. (1978). *Teachers classroom ideologies and notions of the person - world relationship*. Paper for SSRC Sponsored, Conference on Teachers and Pupil Strategies, held at St. Hilda's, Oxford.

Seabrook, J. (1976). *A lasting relationship: Homosexuals and society*. Allen Lane.

Shaw, C. R. (1930). *The jack roller*. University of Chicago Press.

Smith, L., et al. (1985). *A longitudinal nested systems model of innovation and change in schooling*. Mimeo.

Smith, L. (1980). *Archival case records: Issues and illustrations*. Paper presented for SSRC sponsored Case Records Conference, York.

Smith, L., & Geoffrey, W. (1968). *The complexities of an urban classroom*. New York: Holt, Rinehart and Winston.

Smith, L., & Keith, P. (1971). *Anatomy of an educational innovation*. New York: Wiley.

Terkel, S. (1975). *Working*. Allen Lane.

Thomas, W. I., & Znaniecki, F. (1927). *The polish peasant in Europe and America* (2nd ed.). New York.

Thompson, P. (1978). *The voices of the past: Oral history*. Opus.

Thrasher, F. M. (1928). *The gang: A study of 1,313 gangs in Chicago*. University Press, Chicago Press.

Wirth, L. (1928). *The ghetto*. University of Chicago Press.

Woods, P. (1979). *The divided school*. RKP.

Woods, P. (1980a). *Pupil strategies*. Croom Helm.

Woods, P. (1980b). *Teacher strategies*. Croom Helm.

Woods, P., & Hammersley, M. (Eds.). (1977). *School experience*. Croom Helm.

Wright Mills, C. (1959). *The sociological imagination*. Oxford University Press.

Zorbaugh, H. V. (1929). *The gold coast and the slum: A sociological study of Chicago's near North side*. University of Chicago Press.

A GUIDE TO LIFE HISTORY INTERVIEWS

Ivor Goodson

In this chapter a procedural plan for developing life history interviews is described. There are of course many ways to conduct life story interviews but in the preparation of life history interviews, there are a number of stages in the development of the study:

1) GENERAL PROCEDURAL ISSUES

There are a range of procedural issues which need to be considered for those employing life history methods. They actually cover a spectrum of possibilities, but here I have presented them in bi-polar opposition to stress the distinctions:
- Interviewer's questions   versus   Silence
- Structure   versus   Emergence
- Prescription   versus   Freedom
- Interview   versus   Conversation
- Research   versus   Therapy
- Coverage   versus   Depth
- Flow   versus   Focus
- Structure   versus   Emergence
- Prescription   versus   Freedom

'Questions versus silence' is a rather extreme way to present a choice. For it is true that no interview will proceed without some explanation, conversation and some questioning. But I pose the issue this way to challenge a common assumption that the life history interviewer should ask a set of questions. In my experience, the best life history interviews are often those with the least interviewer questions in them. Too often, a question leads back to the interviewer and away from the life storyteller's concerns. Questions which are answered as the life story unfolds provide better answers than those given to specific questions.

As researchers (and like all human beings!), we like to be in control, to feel we are getting the data we want. Paradoxically, this often leads to poorer data, so let me propose a rule:

*The **more** we prescribe our questions, the **more** we structure our enquiries before the interview, the **less** we will learn.* (See I. Goodson and P. Sikes)

This is I think a hard lesson to learn and a hard rule to operate. We are trained as social scientists and as academics to ask questions and to interrogate our subjects.

In life history work, the aim is to get the subject talking and above all to **listen** closely. Always remember, if questions that are crucial are not answered in their own time by the life storyteller, they can always be asked later (just keep a running note of them on your pad as questions emerge and return to them later). This is not to say that a well-timed question will not help – it often will – but the point is to help the life storyteller to tell **their** story, not to get them to help you tell **your** story or answer **your** questions.

| Flow | ↔ | Focus |
| Coverage | ↔ | Depth |

The same balance of concerns should inform decisions about focus and coverage, and the development of flow and depth. When a transcript of a life history interview is produced, it is easy to see if the life storyteller is 'flowing' (M. Csikszentmihalyi, 1991) or deepening. There is a fluency to the story and one can see how the teller is in touch with their deep sense of themselves and their storylines. Normally, the interviewer only provides the occasional 'prompt' or question. Meanwhile, the 'story' proceeds with its own rhythm and integrity. In a sense, this fluency should not be surprising to us – human beings are storytelling animals. All the time we are relearning our own stories, trying them out with others and ourselves. Our story is a practised part of ourselves. The task of the interviewer is to tap into this ongoing narrative flow which is part of the living condition, not to keep interrupting it with our own questions and stories.

2) SELECTING YOUR INFORMANTS

To some extent, this will depend on whether a full life history, a thematic life history or an occupational life history are being undertaken, but normally it is important to establish a spectrum of interviewees. Sometimes this can be achieved by conducting an initial survey to pinpoint the diversity of cases and themes to be examined. An alternative strategy is to conduct a series of pilot interviews in order to establish the spectrum of cases and themes under review.

It is always important not to simply choose informants who appeal to one's own instinctive story lines or sympathies. This is a fairly common complaint about life history: that the life history interviewer chooses informants who are effectively telling his or her own story. For example, in teachers' life histories, often the more pioneering or innovative teachers are chosen. It is less common for the more conformist or conservative teacher to be chosen. This is often because the interviewer may be a past teacher has moved into an academic position and stories his/her experiences as that of a pioneer or innovator. So defining a spectrum of life history informants is a very important first stage.

3) SETTING THE SCENE

A subsequent stage is what might be called 'setting the scene'. Often little thought is given to the scene in which the life history interview will be conducted, but it is of enormous importance. For example, in a recent life history workshop, two women who did not know each other decided to sit facing a picture, rather than facing each other, as a way of easing their way into the interview. The advantage of sitting side-by-side is that you can slowly turn to each other when you are ready to make eye contact, rather than insist upon it from the beginning. If you insist upon it from the beginning, it forces the situation, which to these two women would have felt very unnatural. Lawrence Stenhouse, an early English ethnographer, once argued that the best way to conduct interviews was driving in a car. This way, the interviewer again is looking out of the window ahead and only occasionally turns to make eye contact with the interviewee – likewise, the interviewee is freed from the immediate, interrogative eye of the interviewer. But the setting of the scene for the interviewer is a highly personal decision that has great impact on the subsequent interview. It relates to the next stage of the process.

4) BUILDING TRUST WITH EACH OTHER

Building trust with the interviewee is an incredibly complicated process and has to be established fairly quickly if the interview is to be successfully conducted. That is the problem: you have got to quickly come to a bonding with each other; quickly come to some kind of agreement; quickly develop some sense of intimacy and trust, before there is going to be any proper exchange of views. It is not going to happen if you do not build up intimacy and trust. There is no programmatic way for establishing intimacy and trust: it is a question of human chemistry and, as such, there is no procedural formula.

What is clear, however, is that the more one explains the process and use of the life history interview, the better this is in building early trust. I always make a point of explaining what is going to happen to the interview when it is completed, and explaining what it is for. Often this transaction can be conducted around the signing of an 'informed consent' protocol. The explanation of this protocol can be part of the process of building up trust and intimacy.

5) USING A TAPE RECORDER OR NOTES

I am a very strong believer in the tape recorder for the reason that I think if you do not use a tape recorder, you are constantly breaking eye contact, and if you have worked hard to establish intimacy and trust, this puts you back to the starting point each time.

This does not, however, mean I only use the tape recorder. I also jot down notes as the interview proceeds. For instance, when bigger ideas begin to emerge, it is important to note them down, for they may not come back to you when you do the subsequent transcriptions. So I tend to keep a few quick notes about big ideas as they emerge, and return to them immediately after the interview and fill out my reflections. The negotiation around the use and location of the tape recorder is itself a further part of the process of building up intimacy and trust and setting a personalised scene for the interview to take place.

6) TRANSCRIPTION

It is very important to think hard about who does the transcription at the interview. A common procedure is to put out transcription to a research assistant or secretarial assistant. In general, I would argue this is a bad move. My own experience is that doing the transcription oneself and doing it fairly quickly after the interview, recreates the scene of the interview very adequately and causes a flow of complimentary ideas to come up as you transcribe. It is another way of following up the initial process noted above of reflecting on ideas as they emerge, but I find transcription itself is an important 'trigger' to note emergent themes.

7) DESCRIBING THE SCENE

Often when interview material is presented in reports, the scene of the interview is not fully described. It is important, therefore, to describe the fact that while the interview is being conducted, you were, for example, sitting in front of a picture at this point in time, and at this stage in the afternoon. So you have to imagine the setting, imagine the two people looking at the picture, and you have a sense of how the interview is conducted and the data generated. This is imperative in life history work because this full contextual picture is part of the textual material being presented.

8) ANALYSING TRANSCRIPTS

There are a number of strategies for analysing life history interviews. Noblit and Hare (1988) describe a process of translation and synthesis in developing meta-ethnographics that pursue general topics and concepts; Glaser and Strauss (1967) describe the process of emergent thematising, as do Strauss and Corbin (1990); Patton (1980); Denzin and Lincoln (1984) talk of 'saturation' as their preferred analytic strategy.

In developing a detailed analysis, I adopt a process of immersion, or what I call 'bathing in the data'. I read and re-read the transcripts noting emergent and then recurrent themes; organising the quotes into clusters. Then the clustered quotes on particular topics are analysed again and an initial report prepared. From this, a fuller and more final text can be developed.

Pauses and silences

Bathing in the data often provides surprises and discoveries and should be approached in a manner of open curiosity; predilections and predictions will only limit the potential for themes to emerge. At its best, bathing in the data can be an exciting form of detective work.

The absolutely crucial importance of pauses must be represented in the transcript. What they indicate is that 'this is a difficult question'; 'something important is being asked here'; 'I have got something important to say, but I may not want to say it'. How you indicate pauses in the transcripts is that you should actually time pauses and along the side of the transcript, there should be a timeline indicating the scale of the pause. The question of pauses is related in some senses to the issue of silences. What I mean by silence is the parts of the life and work that are omitted in the descriptions given by the life history teller. For instance, many men talk primarily about their work when giving a life history interview. What is often silent is any discussion of their emotional or familial life. Here the 'silence' is saying something very important about the way that the man is storying his life, or at least is choosing to present that story to a wider audience. It is important for the life history interviewer to note and respect the 'silence' before possibly asking questions about it. This act of interviewer restraint is quite difficult to hold onto sometimes. Let me give an example.

I was interviewing a black middle-aged teacher from Belize in Central America. The interviews took place over a period of three days and in the evening, I was talking to an anti-racist educator, Barry Troyna, who kept saying to me 'why don't you ask him about his colour? Why don't you ask him about his experience of racism?' My response was to say that I needed to restrain myself for a while to allow him to provide me with his own image of himself.

When I did finally ask the question about colour, it became clear that he had always seen himself, until he moved to Canada, as essentially a 'white person'. This was because he had been educated at an English public school in Belize by white Englishmen and had formed a particular image of himself. Interestingly, it was only when he went to teach the Innuits in Northern Canada that he confronted his own colour. So, in this case, interviewer restraint was important to allow the silences around this issue to emerge before, in due course, confronting them. So one lesson from this story is that the interviewer should not rush to fill the silences and spaces that emerge in an interview but should record and respect them before possibly, in due course, seeking to understand them and ask questions about them.

9) 'BUT' ANALYSIS

Another very important aspect of analysis is to focus on the 'buts' and 'howevers' in a text. I would suggest going right through the transcript and ringing in the 'buts' to see if there is anything in 'but' analysis. A good deal of work has been written about how it is important to study the phrases that follow the words 'but' and 'however'. Often these qualifications that come in the text show important changes of direction in the thinking of the life history teller and important qualifications, or alternative visions, that underpin the primary storyline that is being told. This is a point where sometimes a more deviant life history story can be glimpsed beneath the more conformist storyline. It is also a point where the interviewer might 'interrupt subjectivity' to pursue some of these alternative visions and disrupt what might be a rather rehearsed conventional storyline to glimpse something more multi-faceted and complex.

10) FEEDBACK

This is I think in some ways is the most important and neglected part of the process of life history interviewing. Feedback begins when you have transcribed the tape of the first interview, and you have kept a record of your own emergent theoretical ideas and themes, which you have not fed back. It may be that you are planning a second interview to follow up the initial interview and feed back is absolutely crucial now in terms of giving back the knowledge; giving back the transcript, and giving back some of your thoughts about the initial interview. My sense is that people do very different things with what you feed back to them. Sometimes people just correct the grammar; sometimes people think it is just fine as it is, and sometimes they change everything – that can be very interesting: whole sections are sometimes changed – or occasionally, some will come back and say, 'I will not have that part used'. One interviewee that I passed the transcript back to, went through the whole interview introducing mentions of her husband who had been left out entirely in the original transcript – I think this omission said something! If a second interview is being pursued, and this is normally the pattern as life story moves to life history, then the transcript comes back to the interviewer with any comments made by the life story teller. This helps with the process of preparing for the second interview. This second interview is when you try to move the life story into something more like a fully grounded life history. In moving to the life history, as well as the transcript, the interviewer may have done other work – talking to other people; documentary searches; a perusal of policy documents, etc. – so, in this sense, the interviewer is doing triangulation ahead of the second session, because the second interview is really the chance to get the full picture of the person's life history. The second interview is the time when interviewer intuition should be maximised. You have to be absolutely on top of linguistic sensitivity and cultural competence, and this is your opportunity to get whole portrayal of the life history. Obviously, after the second interview, there is another transcription and then there is the writing up of the whole report. That report is the full life history, together with the emergent themes and theories that have emerged during the course of the two interviews. What is presented is essentially a person's life story, fully understood in its historical context.

Once again, after the second interview, you feed back your full life history report, and this is the chance for the person to make further changes before this report is put out into the public domain. Once again, you are giving the chance to the person to question what you came up with; to think about issues of anonymity; to think about issues whether they want this to appear in the public domain. Even at this stage, there should be a power of veto because, of course, the life history teller should have control of their own life material up until this latest point. The reason for the researcher alarm is, of course, that having put in so much time, the prospect of a late veto is alarming. In my experience, in at least 95% of the cases, the veto is not exercised and the report goes out pretty much as it is. You might have a few changes, but if you have done your work properly, this is not a dramatically difficult process.

REFERENCES

Csikszentmihalyi, M. (1991). *Flow: The psychology of optimal experience.* New York: Harper and Row.

Denzin, N. K., & Lincoln, Y. S. (Eds.). (1994). *Handbook of qualitative research.* Thousand Oaks, CA: Sage.

Glaser, B., & Strauss, A. (1967). *The discovery of grounded theory: Strategies for qualitative research.* Chicago: Aldine De Gruyter.

Goodson, I. F., & Sikes, P. (2001). *Life history research in educational setting: Learning lives.* Buckingham and Philadelphia: Open University Press.

Noblit, G. W., & Hare, R. D. (1988). *Meta-ethnography: Synthesizing qualitative studies.* Newbury Park: Sage Publication.

Patton, M. Q. (1980). *Qualitative evaluation methods.* Beverly Hills: Sage.

Strauss, A., & Corbin, J. (1990). *Basics of qualitative research: Grounded theory procedures and techniques.* Newbury Park, CA: Sage Publications.

USING LIFE STORY DATA: STORYLINES, SCRIPTS AND SOCIAL CONTEXT

Ivor Goodson

The use of life stories, life histories and narrative in teacher education is currently a strongly emerging field of enquiry and one with exciting possibilities for reformulating some of the existing paradigms of educational study. There are, however, a number of question marks that immediately arise in scrutinizing stories. One of the issues I want to focus on in this chapter is the question of the "prior script" on which stories are based. For stories do not free themselves of the prior script and predilections which are a feature of all our social enquiries and accounts.

It should be noted that this prior script works in both chronological directions. A script as we know defines and gives meanings to our future actions but likewise social storylines work backwards too. As Schachtel (1959) has noted we tend to recall and remember what the social order signifies as important 'perception and experience themselves develop increasingly into the rubber stamps of conventional clichés' (Schachtel 1959, p.288).

The power of prior script is most clearly evident of course in the work of actors. But sometimes actors themselves take over as the authors of "reality". Take the B-picture actor called Ronald Reagan who went on to become President. In reviewing Reagan's capacity to suspend reality, as Shultz puts it he "did not believe that what happened had, in fact, happened." Reagan in short developed a script to live and work from. Shultz says, "He would go over the 'script' of an event, past or present, in his mind, once that script was mastered, that was the truth - no fact, nor argument, no plea for reconsideration would change his mind." (Draper, 1993, p.59) For Reagan, the script was reality, and given his power, reality was the script. Draper notes "in effect, the grade-B pictures actor was still a grade-B pictures actor as president. He followed a script, because that was what he had learned to do". (p.59)

In general, although most people are not actors and although people tell their stories in personal idiosyncratic ways, they employ prior scripts derived from the general cultural milieu. In this way, they both tell their own story but also narrate it according to wider stories. It is, in short, the relationship between agency and structure as it impinges on the world of storying and narrative.

To explain this interface, let me begin with an example. In much of North American life, the life story as told, if not as lived, follows a series of clear stages. As any Budweiser commercial will tell you, the adult life story opens with a period of feverish enjoyment during our youthful years which begin around 14 and go on as long as they can be sustained. The collision between this view of life as exuberant youth and the indisputable (but heavily contested) acceptance that we die, normally comes with the invented episode of the midlife crisis. In Levinson's (1978) book *Seasons of a Man's Life* (which focuses very narrowly, not only does he focus only on men but on professional men), he narrates the life story as moving from youth to the articulation of a "central dream". Men strive to achieve this dream and the point of culmination, collision or collapse is somewhere around forty. This is followed whether you succeed in your dream or not by the notion of midlife crisis.

What follows this period in most narratives and most stories that are told is the beginning of a period of decline and deterioration culminating in the end of life.

Now in many ways this narrative of youth followed by a central professional dream followed by decline has represented in a reasonable way the life span which was to be expected up until the nineteen fifties or sixties. With the transformation of medical science and the broadening of life expectancy, these prior scripts, these story lines have become anachronistic. However, such is the time lag in redrawing these prior scripts that many life stories are still related in this way. Since the script is anachronistic, its powerful time lag effect shows the continuing power of cultural stories to overlay and overlap our more personal modes of storying.

It is only very recently that literature has begun to provide a non-declining story of life for those people between forty and sixty. As Margaret Gullette (1988) has recently argued in her elegant study of the invention of the midlife progress novel:

the difference in the late twentieth century is that the more optimistic minority view of the life course is beginning to appear, in the reiterated and gradually more self-conscious way that lets any new vision become visible. We are seeing the new paradigm - the new ideology - about the middle years shape itself under our reading eyes" (p.24).

The new ideology, the new prior script speaks about a period of progress rather than decline through the years forty to sixty.

She says:

perhaps, to have life-course sequences for a progressive kind in any numbers we had to wait until several favouring circumstances combined in the second half of the twentieth century. Confessional literature became acceptable, while the novel form provided the illusion of privacy for authors who might otherwise have been reticent to appear more confessional even than the poets (p.26).

Secondly, she argues:

a demographic boom provided an audience getting readier, as it aged, to relinquish its original cult of youth; and thus prepared to hear better news about its anxious aging. Indeed, like Juggernaut, some part of the midlife cohort is happy to crush old stereotypes of aging beneath its future-breasting cart. A postcard, a sweatshirt, and a mug keep before us a progressive slogan: 'Never trust anyone over ~~30, 36, 40,~~ 45'. Where economic decline would have placed an intolerable strain on the reading public's willingness to assent to stories of midlife improvement, the post-war years have been a period of economic boom. Divorce laws and sexual revolution have expanded the choices and attitudes open to adults, and the feminist revolution those open to women, (p.26).

What Gullette is, therefore, hinting at, is that only now is literature, and literature is normally ahead of other cultural carriers of ideology, providing us with a different script for the way we story our life.

The way these storylines are now being taken up can be adequately observed in the way women now talk about their lives. Angela Lambert (1994) recently talked about this in her newspaper column:

Over the last few decades, largely triggered by feminism, there has been a real revolution in the lives of middle-aged women. My mother was typical of her generation: middle-aged at 35, old at 40. I can still remember how poignantly, on her 40th birthday, she wept - as though all the fun had gone out of her life. I'm old, was her cry; nobody will be interested in me, flirt with me, dance with me, ever again.

It didn't cross my mind to think like that at 40, nor yet at 50, nor do I suppose it will at 60. Today's older women can have lives as vigorous and involved in the world and their jobs as older men. That central role is reflected in their faces: full of interest, energy, curiosity and confidence. My female contemporaries look wonderful. They have far too much intelligence to make themselves ridiculous by trying to look girlish, but what they do have is the beauty of an assured style, and control over their own lives (*Lambert*, June 1, 1994, p.17).

Do, please, write a story of how a young man, the son of a serf, who has been a shop boy, a chorister, pupil of a secondary school, and a university graduate, who has been brought up to respect rank and to kiss the priest's hand, to bow to other people's ideas, to be thankful for each morsel of bread, who has been thrashed many a time, who has had to walk about tutoring without galoshes, who has fought, tormented animals, has been fond of dining at the house of well-to-do relations, and played the hypocrite both to God and man without any need but merely out of consciousness of his own insignificance - describe how that young man squeezes the slave out of himself, drop by drop and how, awakening one fine morning, he feels running in his veins no longer the blood of a slave but a genuine human blood (Hoggart, 1958, p. 241).

For my part I am very sorry for him. It is an uneasy lot at best, to be what we call highly taught and yet not to enjoy: to be resent at this great spectacle of life and never to be liberated from a small hungry shivering self. George Eliott (p. 241)

From these quotes Hoggart begins his exploration of the agony and the ecstasy of the scholarship boy. Writing in 1958 he must be situated in a time and place where in Britain socialist governments had been trying to build a post-war 'New Jerusalem' based on certain selective versions of social justice and equity. The 'scholarship boy' story then stands testimony to a particular version of the progress narrative - one which now stands disvalued as reminiscent of outmoded models of meritocracies, masculinisms and marxisms. These factors give Hoggart's text a strangely dated flavour even though he was writing less than forty years ago.

It will be convenient to speak first of the nature of the uprooting which some scholarship boys experience. I have in mind those who, for a number of years, perhaps for a very long time, have a sense no longer really belonging to any group. We all know that many do find a poise in their new situations. There are 'declassed' experts and specialists who go into their own spheres after the long scholarship climb has led them to a Ph.D. There are brilliant individuals who become fine administrators and officials, and find themselves thoroughly at home. There are some, not necessarily so gifted, who reach a kind of poise which is yet not a passivity nor even a failure in awareness, who are at ease in their new group without any ostentatious adoption of the protective colouring of that group, and who have an easy relationship with their working-class relatives, based not on a form of patronage but on a just respect. Almost every working-class boy who goes through the process of further education by scholarships finds himself chafing against his environment during adolescence. He is at the friction-point of two cultures; the test of his real education lies in his ability, by about the age of twenty-five, to smile at his father with his whole face and to respect his flighty young sister and his slower brother. I shall be concerned with those for whom the uprooting is particularly troublesome, not because I under-estimate the gains which this kind of selection gives, nor because I under-estimate the gains which this kind of selection gives, nor because I wish to stress the more depressing features in contemporary life, but because the difficulties of some people illuminate much in the wider discussion of cultural change. Like transplanted stock, they react to a widespread drought earlier than those who have been left in their original soil.

I am sometimes inclined to think that the problem of self-adjustment is, in general, especially difficult for those working-class boys who are only moderately endowed, who have talent sufficient to separate them from the majority of their working-class contemporaries, but not to go much farther. I am not implying a correlation between intelligence and lack of unease; intellectual people have their own troubles: but this kind of anxiety often seems most to afflict those in the working-classes who have been pulled one stage away from their original culture and yet have not the intellectual equipment which would then cause them to move on to join the 'declassed' professionals and experts. In one sense, it is true, no one is ever 'declassed'; and it is interesting to see how this occasionally obtrudes (particularly today, when ex-working-class boys move in all the managing areas of society) - in the touch of insecurity, which often appears as an undue concern to establish 'presence' in an otherwise quite professional professor, in the intermittent rough homeliness of an important executive and committee-man, in the tendency to vertigo which betrays a lurking sense of uncertainty in a successful journalist. (pp. 242-243)

The scholarship boy's script was employed by a wide range of young men in a variety of different social situations. I have previously written of my own experience of this but here it is important to focus on the enormous 'outreach' of this prior script. What follows is a life story narrated by a fifty year old black male teacher who grew up in Belize in Central America. Besides its importance in analyzing the prior scripting of storylines it is valuable as an introduction to the texture of life story narrations:

I suppose that the significant figures that we looked up to were always educated people. Not sports figures or particularly wealthy people who had made their mark by amassing vast fortunes. When I was growing up, we had a notion of what a good job was: always a job with the civil service. This was British Colonial rule and the civil service was very attractive to us because you got to wear a nice clean white shirt and a tie to go to work, as opposed to coming out from under the bottom of a car all grimy and besmirched. But, of course, for a civil service job you need at least a high school education. But in Belize, where I was growing up a high school education was not a foregone conclusion. You had to pay for high school unless you won a government scholarship. It wasn't a case of applying; everyone who went to elementary school would take the government scholarship exam in grade six. I'm not sure exactly what standards they applied but very few people won those scholarships. I distinctly recall, because it was a significant item in my life, that there were thirty three of us in my grade six class, and I was the only one who got a scholarship. There was also a church scholarship, but in order to win it you had to be a regular churchgoer. I also won a church scholarship, together with another pupil, James Roby. Apparently, I had done slightly better than him. I distinctly remember our meeting with some "authority figures", who explained to me that this was James's last chance because he was older than I was, and that I had a very good chance of getting a government scholarship. When I went to St. Paul's College, the Anglican high school I attended, which was run according to the British system, with forms, there were about twenty five to thirty of us in the first form. There were about five scholarship winners, but these had come from all over the country. They were all Anglicans, of course. The others were paid for by their parents. The government scholarship was a good thing, because your family just had to provide the uniform: Khaki shorts or long pants, a white shirt with short sleeves and a green tie. The school sold the tie. We all went around with green ties, white shirts and khaki pants. When I look back now it cuts a funny sort of picture, but at that time it was a significant move in your life. At that time, we felt privileged to go to high school, because for many of our elementary classmates, that was it --grade six. In Belize, parents, regardless of a child's academic potential, always felt that a son should have some sort of trade to fall back on. So during my elementary years, along with, I suppose, all my contemporaries, went to learn a trade. My mother packed my younger brother and myself off to a tailor. But in my mind, even though I was very young, I knew very well that I was not going to be a tailor. I didn't know what I was going to be, but I was not going to sit in some gloomy tailors shop and sew clothes for people all my life, and come out hunch backed after twenty years of this, looking for and picking up pieces of thread. I wasn't going to do that: it would be too stultifying. I suppose way back then I saw myself as an academic person. As it turned out, this was confirmed by my experiences. I did very well in elementary school, I suppose it's the same all over the world, doing well in high school does a whole lot for yourself esteem and your popularity. People respect you because you are smart, and that meant all kinds of things. For example, one of the so called smart things I displayed was the ability to memorise things. The school always put on plays, and my fantastic memory enabled me to get parts. I was very well respected --Johnson, he's very smart, he's got a future -- that type of thing. I remember, earlier than grade four, that I was taken to some classroom where there were some other people, and we had to do a little test. The end result was that I skipped grade five, and went from grade four into grade six. I was very young in grade six. During the first couple of recesses, an old grade four classmate taunted me with: get away from me, you smart Alec! It's funny how we remember these things while forgetting what happened more recently. My school experiences have always been imprinted on my mind. They were always really encouraging experiences because I was so enthusiastic and so keen. Teachers loved me. When I look back now this was inevitable, I got along with them quite well. In grade four you have a crush on your teacher, and I distinctly recall having a crush on this teacher, Miss Janet Jones. She liked me very much. My big thrill was that I would go to her house on Saturdays and wash her bicycle. Bicycles, then, were the way of getting around, and as a result, people took exceedingly good care of them. They would polish them and clean every spoke. After I had washed her bicycle, I could ride it. So there I was, quite proudly tooling around the city riding Miss Jones's bicycle. In a different environment it would be the equivalent of a teacher lending a car. We didn't have bicycles ourselves, so I would visit my classmates and friends -- they knew I was riding teacher's bicycle. Education officers visited our school, and they appeared to us as powerful figures. They went beyond the white shirt and tie to suit jackets. Very nice. To us, these guys were the pinnacle of professional achievement. We looked up to them.

After that, it was on to St. Paul's College. That was also a very good experience as I continued to be quite enthusiastic and hard working. St. Paul's College had speech night at the end of every school year. There was a prize for every subject area. Of course, being the academic, highly competitive person I was, I always tried to get a couple of prizes, and always did, at least win something. I never forget how proud I always made my mother, God rest her soul. It was her son, and this is St. Paul's College. I mean, after all we are talking about a place that had no university. Years after I graduated from high school, there was still no university, which is why I didn't go to university until I left the country. Of course, some people did stick their noses to the grindstone and go to University from there, but I didn't. Speech night was very important because in a class of twenty or thirty boys, two or three would be getting all the prizes. It wasn't that spread out because it was mainly an Arts School: History, Geography, Language, Health Science, Mathematics-- but Algebra and Physical Geometry, not Trigonometry, no Science. Our school didn't have a science programme at all. Later on, when the government opened a technical school in the north part of the city, some of us were encouraged, because they thought we could do it, half way along, to drop a couple of subjects from our regular curriculum. So, for example, I dropped Health Science and Geography and in the evenings I went over to this school and took Chemistry and Physics. But, anyway, that programme didn't work out well because we were well along in our exercises when we had to take the GCE. At that time it was called the Cambridge School Certificate. High school was very enjoyable. A person who has been a prominent person in my life is my high school English teacher, Howard Robinson. He has since gone on to be one of the outstanding intellectuals in the country. He received his B.A. in English from U.C.W., and his Ph.D., with a thesis on the Creole language as spoken in Belize, in England. He was my mentor throughout my high school years.

After I finished high school I got into teaching. At that time you could enter teaching in two different ways. You could stay on after elementary school and become a teacher's aid, then by taking exams, obtain your first class teacher's certificate. This would take about five years. Alternatively, you could teach once you completed high school. I graduated high school in November and started teaching in January. It makes sense, as far as content is concerned. You certainly learn enough in high school to teach elementary school. In university Ph.D.s teach M.A. There's not that much difference. Once I started teaching, I did in-service-training, with courses in methodology, psychology, and class room methods and management. I travelled to the district capital once or twice a week to attend classes. After two years I received my first class teacher's certificate. About that time a teacher's college opened, but most who went there didn't have high school. I think there was certain elitist attitude there about high school. I taught elementary for three years from the time I was eighteen. ...I taught elementary for three years in two rural schools. In the second I was the vice-principal. An older woman was the principal and I think the powers that be wanted me to stay on and eventually take over the school. But I don't think it was meant to be; I didn't see that as what I really wanted to do. I didn't know what I wanted to do, but I think that way back in my head was always the notion that I would leave Belize, and that I would never want to stay there. It always struck me that it was a place that would eventually end up being quite stifling. That may not be so. I know a lot of my ex-classmates who ended up getting a university education and are quite well placed and they seem to love it. But I think I'm the kind of person who prefers to swim in a larger pond.

Even though I might be anonymous in that pond, than to rule in a very, very, small little puddle and to move in a sort of almost claustrophobic world. That had never appealed to me. Education is very important in Belize. There is one radio station, Radio Belize. Since there was no university there, anyone leaving the country to study was a news item. The radio would announce: departing from Belize Airport today is A, son of B and C of 1 D street, he is making his way to E to study R. Then four years later, when he returned the event was announced. Conquering Hero. This was a very important thing, because in a country where high school education couldn't be taken for granted, a person with a degree was a deity, really! You could get a degree in anything and be considered super smart. So when a person returned to Belize International Airport! Even Cambridge School Certificates were announced on the radio. Students from all over the country got together in Belize City to take the exam in this huge hall, with proctors walking up and down. The exams were then sent to England to be graded and marked. Several months later the results were announced on Radio Belize, they would state the school and the class of the certificate. This radio station was the only one in the whole country, education is a very powerful thing to Belizeans; they give education very high value. You want to be one of those announced on the radio for passing your school certificate, and, maybe, one day announced as departing the International Airport. I'm just making this connection right now, this powerful thing, imagining the poor guys who didn't make it through high school. You know there is a certain class there, there's a definite thing, you either have a high school education or you don't! You either have a university education or you do not. It's like that. It's funny though, much as they had a university education, obviously something I dreamed of in a way, my not having a university education made it seem too out of reach for me. Because if you wanted to go to university, there were two ways of doing it, you could win a government scholarship or you could have your parents pay for you. Our family couldn't afford it, in fact if I had not won a scholarship to high school I wouldn't have had a high school education. (Interview, George, 1992, pp.1-6)

In the initial narration, George Johnson provides a rich commentary on the power of the scholarship boy script in organizing a life story. As with Reagan we note how in a real sense the script of a life story narration represents reality in certain ways. If we view the self and identity as ongoing narrative projects we begin to see the sheer power of the script in organizing and representing reality - both to the self and to others.

But as we noted earlier, the recent scholarship boy storyline grew out of a social and political milieu of optimistic meritocracy following the Second World War. Resources were limited but growing and for a minority of the working class, there was the potential for social mobility - this potential, this window of opportunity, was celebrated in the scholarship boy story. The scholarship boy represented a particular selectivity of class, gender and race at a particular historical moment.

In the event this moment passed and in hiatus of the sixties was effectively deconstructed. But for those who had scripted their lives on this storyline, the story continued as their chosen representation of reality. One of the fascinations of collaborating on life story narrations is to see how intensive 'grounded conversations' and introspective reflection combine to allow the life story tellers to 'locate' their stories. George Johnson spoke of this process towards the end of collaborating on his life story when historical and sociological insights began to provide the material for him to locate his story.

Looking back, I feel I betrayed the academic promise I showed as a child. Examining the tapes and transcripts had dislodged a number of memories and subsequent feelings. On Monday, I felt quite depressed, I realize that life had passed by. I was troubled by thoughts of what should have been. At this stage I should be a professor or an executive with a house and car. Where have twenty five years gone?

A university degree is very important to me; I always envied those who returned to Belize with one. I appreciate there are complex reasons behind this. Part of me doubts my ability to do university studies. I don't know if I've got what it takes. However, at some point I made choices. I avoided putting my abilities to the test. Although I didn't articulate it at the time, now, on reflection -- I escaped. I chose a different path. I was a womaniser who ignored my intellectual potential. Eventually I chose marriage over studies. Within my own family, my stepfather, a driver, was an incorrigible womaniser. In high school, despite my academic success I was rebellious and made trouble for the teacher, largely through my quick wit. I avoided further education, but felt frustrated. I know perceive leaving St. Paul's for Honduras as running away because I didn't want to be trapped. I knew I wanted a university degree but wasn't prepared to face the challenge so I quit. I didn't want to be edged out; I didn't want to be an anachronism.

Honduras seemed the logical choice since I was born there. I now see this journey as a flight from self, or from destiny. Only by attending university could I be announced: arriving at the airport...I don't really know whether I wanted that, living out a culturally provided script. (Interview, George Johnson, 1992, pp.73-74)

SCRIPTS AND STORYLINES

The examples of mid-life progress narratives and scholarship boy stories show the intimate relationship between social and political circumstances and cultural storylines. In a real sense social structures push storylines in particular directions and the stories then legitimate the structures - and so on in a self legitimating circle. The relationship between social structure and story is loosely-coupled and stories can resist as well as enhance the imperatives of structure. The scholarship boy story is a particular example of this - a 'celebration' of a particular historical moment of opportunity for a selective group of male students sometimes of working class origin. The storyline then privileges some; more significantly, however, it silences the many - as a storyline it silences women, it silences most of the 'non-scholarship' working class and it silences whole nations and racial groups where such windows of opportunity do not exist. With the passing of the scholarship boy, we see the long overdue end of a storyline, but as we have seen when life storylines become obsolescent in the wider cultural setting this leaves a good deal of rehabilitation and reformulation to be undertaken at the level of the narrative project of the self.

The collection of personal and practical stories of teaching has the tendency to convert the inherited social scripts and cultural storylines of teaching. We lose a sense of the social embeddings of teaching of the gendered inheritance of script. As Madeleine Grumet has elegantly inveighed. "When we summon women to adopt a form of practice that is aesthetic [such as teaching], we find that the workplace replicates those structures in domesticity and in female identity that repudiate freedom and action." (Grumet quoted in Willinsky, 1989, p. 252)

Willinsky (1989) has critiqued 'personal practical knowledge' approaches for this denial of wide social context and storyline: "The place of a larger, inherited script may be lost sight of in their efforts to keep close to the performance of the teacher before them".(p. 250) Hence he argues it is the privilege and duty of the externally located researcher that "in serving the teacher in this collaborative project, (we should) describe the history of the script and set within which the teacher is busily improvising and performing".(p. 252)

The collection of stories then, especially the mainstream stories that live out a "prior script", will merely fortify patterns of domination. We shall need to move from life stories to life histories, from narratives to genealogies of context, towards a modality that embraces "Stories of action within theories of context". In so doing stories can be "located", seen as the social constructions they are, fully implicated in their location within power structures and social milieu. Stories then provide a starting point for active collaboration, "a process of deconstructing the discursive practices through which one's subjectivity has been constituted". (Middleton, 1992, p.20) Only if we deal with stories as the *starting point* for collaboration, as the *beginning* of a process of coming to know, will we come to understand their meaning; to see them as social constructions which allow us to locate and interrogate the social world in which they are embedded. As well as the data being distinctive, so too then are the aspirations of life story and life history. In the first case the intention is to understand the person's view and account of their life, the story they tell about their life. As W.I. Thomas said 'if men define situations as real, they are real in their consequences'. In the life history, the intention is to understand the patterns of social relations, interactions and constructions in which the lives of women and men are embedded. The life history pushes the question whether private issues are also public matters, the life story individualises and personalises, the life history contextualises and politicises.

In moving from life stories towards life histories we move from singular narration to include other documentary sources and oral testimonies. It is important to view the self as an emergent and changing 'project' not a stable and fixed entity. Over time our view of ourselves change and so, therefore, do the stories we tell about ourselves. In this sense, it is useful to view self definition as an ongoing narrative project.

As the self is an ongoing narrative project, we should think more of multiple selves located in time and space. To link with this ongoing narrative project, we have to <u>locate</u> as well as narrate since the latter is a snapshot, a contemporary pinpoint. To locate our ongoing narrative requires sources which develop our social history and social geography of circumstances and in many instances collaboration with others to provide contextual and inter-textual commentary. Along side <u>narration</u>, therefore, we need <u>location</u> and <u>collaboration</u>.

The reasons for location and collaboration arise from two particular features of life stories. First, the life story reflects partial and selective consciousness of subjective story building and self-building; and secondly, it is a contemporary pinpoint, a snapshot at a particular time. Collaboration and location allow us to get a finer sense of the emergent process of self-building and story telling and allow us to provide a social context of the time and space in which the story is located. Such work might provide wider understandings both for those involved in the collaborative studies and for those other audiences of readers and interpreters who may review any textual outcomes of these collaborations. In scrutinizing stories, our sense of the teacher's life and work might develop new insights and reflexivities.

REFERENCES

Buruma, I. (1991, February 14). Signs of life. *New York Review of Books, 38*(4).

Denzin, N. K. (1991, April). *Deconstructing the biographical method.* Paper presented at the 1991 AERA Annual Meeting, Chicago, Illinois.

Draper, T. (1993, June 10). Iran-contra: The mystery solved. *New York Review of Books, 40*(11).

Goodson, I. F. (Ed.). (1992). *Studying teachers' lives.* London and New York: Routledge.

Gullette, M. (1988). *Safe at last in the middle years.* Berkeley, Los Angeles, London: University of California Press.

Hogart, R. (1958). *The uses of literacy.* Harmondsworth, Middlesex: Penguin Books in association with Chatto & Windrus.

Lambert, A. (1994, June 1). A very dodgy foundation. In *The Independent.*

Levinson, D. J. (1978). *Seasons of a man's life.* New York: Knopf.

Macintyre, A. (1981). *After virtue. A study in moral theory.* London: Duckworth.

Middleton, S. (1992). Developing a radical pedagogy. In I. F. Goodson (Ed.), *Studying teachers' lives.* London and New York: Routledge.

Naipaul, V. S. (1987). *The enigma of arrival.* London: Viking.

Schachtel, E. (1959). On memory and childhood amnesia. In *Metamorphosis.* New York: Basic Books.

Willinsky, J. (1989). Getting personal and practical with personal practical knowledge. *Curriculum Inquiry, 19*(3).

A PROFESSIONAL LIFE IN REFORMING TIMES

Ivor Goodson

I first met Berry in 1998 in an industrial city in New York State. The initial reason for our meeting was that our research project had begun in the local university and it was my role as research director to devise a research programme, and to look for key informants to further develop that process and provide data and insights. We were looking at the way that the educational system was undergoing reform and change. Rather than writing a conventional report, we had begun to look at the process of organisational change from the viewpoint of those at the end of the change mandates: the teachers, students and parents. As a locally-renowned teacher, Berry, with a stream of distinguished teaching awards and a significant local reputation, offered the chance to see how one of the most committed practitioners felt about the reform and changes sweeping through the district.

Berry's school, Sheldon, had gone through a trajectory recognisable in many downtown areas of New York State. From its origins as a high status comprehensive with a broad social and racial mix and a fine academic reputation, it had faced decline and social turmoil. In the early 1970s, race riots led many of the White families to decide to leave for the suburbs. Sheldon School withstood these changes, but a new magnet initiative promoting school choice and competition began in 1984. This initiative drew many of the most gifted students away from Sheldon, once again reducing the School's academic reputation and also leading to more White students leaving the School. In the same period, the District closed a nearby high school with a high Afro-American clientele, and large numbers of these students and some of the associated staff were transferred to Sheldon. By 1989, half of Sheldon's students were estimated to be living in poverty, and by 2000 this had reached 70 per cent. The School was caught by magnet initiatives which draw academic students away, and by school transfers which brought less academic students into the School.

The period of the 1970s, and especially 1980s, was one of precipitous decline in Sheldon School - a time of growing discipline problems and declining academic performance. Yet, during this period, Berry remained committed to his work in the School and performed at a level that led to many teaching awards for excellence. This was not a teacher easily deflected by social turmoil, by racial dissent; by changing racial composition, or by changing academic priorities. In these years, he continued to stand his ground, to 'build his own classroom world' of excellence and commitment. Indeed, he judged he was at a professional
peak in these years of school decline and deterioration.

I got my creative writing class in 1975 and then I got my first honors class in Y9. From 75, until probably '85, was kind of golden age where the kids I was getting and my own intellectual curiosity were at a peak, and I was living off energy that was coming from outside and inside. And I was constantly looking for new staff, finding new material, building up new staff, and testing things out. And it was a great time period. About 1985, 1986, I think, I entered a period of real competence where I felt like I was someone with tools that I could use well and at will. I was a... I became a much more rigorous teacher.

These statements show Berry as a model professional, working in very difficult conditions in a school with some of the poorest and also most challenging students, but bringing a sense of commitment and mission to the task. He has achieved this by polishing up his own professional skills, by developing his relationships with his students and by constantly replenishing his intellectual and teaching 'resource-bank'. He has built a classroom world full of rich learning experiences full of teaching passion and purpose - a site of commitment and craft. He is practising his commitment to public education, to teaching children of all classes and races, to teaching as a moral craft. For a society under pressure to improve, for the social fabric to be strengthened, for a sense of community to endure, such teachers must be nurtured, strengthened and supported. Such teachers attract and mentor new teachers.

Into Berry's world came new reforms and restructuring initiatives. In the 1980s, the USA experienced a rapid growth of standards-based reform movements. In this School district in the late 1980s, the State mandated competency tests in five subjects. In 1990, these tests were extended to six subjects and the required credits for graduates were expanded from 20.5 in 1986, to 23.5 for entering students a decade later. By this time, in the mid-1990s, a range of testing experiments had been narrowed down to a testing regime tied to the State's standards. Student graduation was dependent on passing standardised tests in five subjects.

Berry's sense of mission and commitment was to be itself tested by the new standards-based reform. But first, we have to establish where Berry's mission originated and how it came to have such a compelling role in his teaching excellence, and in the management of his life 'dream' or 'mission'. Berry graduated in English Literature with a minor in Archive Writing from the University of Louisville in 1968. He had a Creative Writing Scholarship and was editor of the literary magazine and Arts editor of The College newspaper. Upon graduation, not wanting to fight in Vietnam, he joined the Peace Corps and chose to serve in India.

His humanism is evident in that in his first teaching assignment at a school with a rising Afro-American population in a blue-collar area, he quickly felt at home. The School fitted with his liberal notions of treating all students equally in a democracy. This moral purpose and mission, of course goes deep into American history - Horace Mann's Common School – epitomised this democratic ideal and was the precursor to the comprehensive high school, he found himself in. The sixties generation was strongly imbued with such moral purpose, a desire for community and equality and, in that sense, Berry was like any number of men and women who chose teaching as a way of exploring their moral commitment to breathing life into the American democratic project. Of course, this infusion of new life coincided with the demographic bulge of the baby boomers who brought so much change and invention in their wake.

His commitment found an echo in the student community, whether Italian, Polish, White or Afro-American. He valued them all and this quickly created good learning environments in his classroom. He judged that 'the Afro-American kids really liked me. And I think it was just because I was honest and real and so were they'. He also 'realised early on that there were certain things that he did pretty well. I could build up a rapport with a class very quickly; I could get them interested in the literature very quickly'. His belief in social inclusion and his definition of inclusive learning strategies plainly complemented each other and won him a broad student following.

However, as we talked, Berry says how much time and thought goes into his teaching. He is always collecting resources and ideas, ways of involving his students in relevant issues and strategies for motivating them to learn literature. His mission to educate is compulsive, continuous and coherent. So much so, that he always arrives at 5.30 am and spends two hours preparing himself for his lessons. A dedicated professional then, dedicated to education and to spreading that learning as far across the social and racial mosaic of the school community as possible. The aim is to educate all future citizens of the republic: an honourable aim - part of his generation's sense of mission and what it is that motivates him to give his best and to clearly achieve sustained excellence in his classroom.

Teachers with a strong commitment and sense of mission are incredibly valuable assets in any society. Hence, reforms should approach such professionals with some humility and sensitivity. In truth, 'you don't mend it if it ain't broke' and, if it already functions superbly as is the case with Berry, reform should be careful and caring.

Standards-based reform is, however, a blunt instrument, not least because it is standardised, not tailored to the personal and emotional side of teaching, not tuned to listen to the generational missions and commitments which motivate teachers through a lifetime.

Berry's original commitment was to a comprehensive high school that educated all students and aspired to equality of opportunity. Over time; structural changes began to erode such a vision - such erosions are perennial and persistent and inevitable as inequality widens. Magnet School attracted pupils away, suburbs attracted the richer and primarily White parents away; school transfers increased the concentration of poverty and of minority students. As we saw, Berry's teaching accommodated to these setbacks in his classroom; his vision continued and his teaching remained excellent, bringing a stream of awards.

Into this trajectory of structural challenge, met and dealt with in his classroom, come the new reforms which do not stop at the classroom door. This time, Berry himself is to be treated as a standardised performer of tasks, increasingly defined by others. A master craftsman is treated as a technician complying with the dictates of others and closely monitored as to his level of performance.

His testimony as to the effects of the reforms is characteristically precise and honest:

This has been a particularly frustrating, demoralizing school year for me. Classes are so large, the expectations of the district and the school so specific, and the motivations and skills of the students so low that I find myself thinking in terms of period-to-period survival rather than in terms of grand educational success.

Two mandates are hounding me. One is referred to by our district as 'alignment': the development of what used to be called interdisciplinary curricula. I have always used social studies skills and content in my English courses and so I have welcomed 'alignment'. Last year my principal and my department head made sure students' schedules were arranged so that all students in a particular social studies class also had the same English teacher. English and social studies' teachers were expected to work together and developed parallel curricula (as well as deal as a team with individual students' problems).

The plan turned out to be a logistical nightmare and was abandoned, except in the so-called honors classes. I teach tenth grade honors English, so I am still expected to work with my students' social studies' teacher and to develop a curriculum that parallels the 1750 to the modern era syllabus of the global studies IIH course.

One of my first choices was to add A Tale of Two Cities to my course. Out of the 60 students in the class, I would say six actually read the whole book. I had the students keep reading logs - monitoring both their understanding of the text and their own reading processes: where, when, for how long, under what conditions they read? The logs led to no particular insights into the book or into their own thinking processes. They only confirmed my assumption that they couldn't and wouldn't read anything that posed a challenge to them.

At the same time, I am trying to work in the other mandate the district has issued - that we prepare our students for the new Regents exams. Such work is tedious, uninteresting, and time-consuming for both the students and me. The paper load is overwhelming. It is also disruptive to the content and sequencing of the 'alignment' curriculum. Students see 'prepping' for the exam as a disconnected, almost absurd activity.

All the teaching skills I have - skills that have won me five distinguished teaching awards over the last 20 years - seem insufficient to the challenges I have before me....

As a result of these frustrations, I have sunk into a period of depression... Usually, all I need to keep me excited about teaching is a handful of interested students and the freedom to use their interest to engage the rest.

This year, the nuts and bolts of curriculum, paper grading and monitoring of students has left me no time or energy for the more global kind of thinking that charges my battery.

A common explanation purveyed by reformers is that teacher demotivation among established teachers is just a part of ageing. This does not equate with those teachers who have continued to perform stellar work throughout their careers, when they are valued and their purposes and missions accord with the overall societal vision of education. The destruction of Berry's commitment seems of a different order, for his sense of purpose and commitment are palpable, undimmed when you talk with him. This is a man of passion and purpose, but his purposes are at odds with the new vision. His memory of socially inclusive school communities and of egalitarian politics is deliberately contradicted by the new reforms which celebrate successful students in the suburbs and stigmatise the majority of students in the downtown. For the latter groups, standardisation systematises, organises and labels exclusion. These are Berry's students.

At the time, Berry's lifetime of creativity and resourcefulness, his memory of professional life, as based on his judgement and his skill, is undermined. We see a more prescriptive, micro-managed, professional practice replacing the professional patterns in which he excelled and his students profited. No wonder his sense of professional disillusionment is so articulate.

When excellent teachers become disillusioned, this is a problem for standards-based reform. You do not deliver higher standards by disillusioning the excellent teacher: you end up inevitably lowering standards. Standards-based reforms have to develop an understanding of why excellent teachers pursue excellence. These are common threads.

Excellent teachers tend to have an overarching sense of mission and vocation. As we have noted earlier, Levinson, Sheehy, and many others, tell us that most people develop a 'central dream' in their life - a commanding storyline that articulates their passion and purpose into a project or mission around which they organise their life. They judge the success and failures of their lives around the outcome of this central dream or mission.

Reforms which deny, ignore or otherwise disvalue the sense of mission of excellent teachers are therefore counter-productive. It is not only that the excellent teacher is demotivated, but that good role models are demolished and good mentors diminished. The contagion of disillusionment spreads; the notion that teaching is a highly committed vocation on which professional men and women centre their life worlds is destroyed. When mission and meaning are lost, work becomes a more minimal commitment - people start to just turn up and go through the motions. As one new recruit said: 'It's just a job - I turn up, they tell me what to do. I do it and I go home at the earliest opportunity'. This is what you get when you ignore the 'hearts and minds' of excellent teachers and it leads not to rising standards, but overall to falling standards. Were this solely a matter of standards, it would be manageable, but it is behind this a collapse of social purpose and a destruction of more socially inclusive public practices.

TELLING TALES OUT OF SCHOOL

Ivor Goodson and Chris Anstead

Founded in 1912, the London Technical and Commercial High School (later renamed the H.B. Beal Secondary School) marked London's contribution to the vocational movement in education (Anstead and Goodson, 1993a). Representing an alternative model of secondary education in the city, the school was - and remains - a frequent site of contestation. Because of this central role in local educational struggles, a history of the school can be recaptured from a wealth of archival sources. Such a traditional undertaking, however, results in the reconstruction of one particular type of view of the past. In addition, as an investigation moves closer to the contemporary period, documentary sources become less and less available, due to issues of confidentiality, and micro political or political secrecy.

The collection of oral testimonies of this school fills in the gaps in more recent periods; at the same time such accounts can help answer at least part of the challenge to produce a "comprehensive perspective on the actual experience of sitting in a classroom" (Gaffield, 1986 p.116). Yet such an enterprise throws up new questions - the central one of which is: is it possible to reconstruct an ethnographic account of the past, based on interviews with people in the present?

Certainly, a series of interviews with former school students and teachers can lead to a sense of the day-to-day experience of schooling. But this summative story also is marked by two sorts of challenges to an empiricist usage - they may contain mythical elements, and they seem to reflect a collective, socialized, memory. The following sections summarize the narrated experience of schooling as it took place at the school, first in the early 1930s, and then in the late 1960s[1]

EVERYDAY LIFE (1930'S).[2]

When they arrived at school, Depression-era students congregated outside their assigned external doors, with boys at one end of the school, and girls, almost a block away, at the other - starting a segregation of the genders which continued throughout the day. After roll call and morning exercises in the auditorium, commercial and technical students went their separate ways. The structures of school organization allowed for very little mixing between the two groups of students; even non-vocational classes, such as academic subjects or physical training, were taken separately. The same group of students remained together as a class for the whole day, moving as a group from room to room. As the students moved through the halls in single file, teachers would come out to ensure that order was maintained, and that no one was speaking.

Male students in the technical division spent much of their day in shop classes, under teachers who spent most of their time going amongst the fifteen to twenty pupils to check their work. Male students in their first year took classes in the range of specialties available: woodworking, machine shop, electricity, building construction, draughting, motor mechanics, printing and sheet metal work. They were expected to produce a variety of standard projects in each of these subjects. For their second year, male technical students picked one subject in which to specialize, and produced much more complex projects.

Female technical students studied domestic subjects. Their teachers spent a lot of time discussing efficient methods of housekeeping, including particular dusting, sweeping or floor-washing techniques. Sewing class featured various forms of needlework: sewing, crochet, embroidery, and petite-point. The three rooms dedicated to cooking classes each had a couple of big stoves, along with individual burners for students. The teacher would announce the day's work, give a demonstration, and then, depending on the teacher, either sit quietly at the other end of the room, or roam from student to student.

The flamboyant Mrs. Cryderman taught Art - the only technical course open to both males and females. Although she emphasized the fine arts, Cryderman taught more commercial applications, such as sign painting, as well.

In contrast to the variety of trades learned in technical courses, commercial students had to focus on three subjects: typing, shorthand, and bookkeeping. Passing the year depended on adequate speeds in typing and shorthand, so teachers ran a lot of drills and tests for speed.

Pupils from both sections of the school took academic subjects as well. Most of the teachers started each class by putting the day's work on the board, and then went up and down the aisles to check each student's progress, and, often, to confirm that they had done the assigned homework. A teacher who wished to include any additional information as part of the lesson, delivered it in the form of a lecture while standing at the front of the room.

Not every teacher followed this plan; the English teachers in particular tended to employ a different teaching style, inviting class discussions, which sometimes led to "pretty hot arguments" (Walsh). One teacher encouraged his students to further immerse themselves in Shakespeare's plays, to the point of having some of the boys fence with yardsticks at the front of the room.

Students in every course took physical training, though classes did not take place as frequently as for other subjects. Most PT classes were spent either in floor games (like basketball) or, more frequently, in gymnastic exercises - doing exercises, running, tumbling or using various pieces of equipment. One student recalled:

> Our gym teacher...was an ex-Royal Navy man....He had a cane - a bamboo cane - he called his 'persuader.'...Now they had ropes tied to the roof of the gym, and you went up them hand over hand. He'd always demonstrate it first,

and then you were expected to go up those ropes. Eventually, [you were expected] to get up there at the same time as he could, and if you didn't make it, he'd let you go so far and then you'd get a whack across the rump with the 'persuader' (Kennedy).

Despite the teachers' efforts, not all students conformed to their idea of disciplined behaviour. One of the most popular means of misbehaviour was to throw things (peanuts for instance) at the teacher when his or her back was turned. Writing rude things on the blackboards or other places in the classroom also proved popular. Students in many courses would try to get away with practical jokes, though the technical students usually had the most access to materials which could serve their pranks. Thus students in the auto mechanics course would take some carbide (used in early automobile lamps) and drop it into water to generate an awful, pervasive, odour (Cushman).

The day's round of classes was broken by the lunch hour. After completing their meals, students left the school building and mixed with their friends, often walking the streets of downtown London for an hour or so.

While students spent their school day in the company of the same group of classmates (usually of the same gender), extracurricular sports and activities allowed students from different years, different classes and different courses to meet. The annual school shows, for instance, involved hundreds of students, including a large cast, the orchestra, and scores of workers.

Dances were a regular fixture of the social calendar. As the school orchestra played waltzes, foxtrots or jitterbugs, the teachers - acting as chaperons - would lead by example and dance themselves. Even here, young men and women acknowledged the strict adolescent social rules which governed their behaviour:

There'd be a line of boys along one wall and a line of girls along the other wall.... They wouldn't think anything of going over and asking a girl to dance. The girls...didn't ever ask the boys. The girls were not aggressive.... You waited 'till a boy asked you. If you didn't get asked you were considered a 'wallflower' (Geddes).

As they sat between dances, students would talk of many things - including their views of the school. Frequently the discussion turned to P.J. Fallona, a fairly new teacher who already had a reputation as a stern disciplinarian. Apparently, a group of senior boys had recently taken exception to Fallona's approach. They had picked him up, pushed him out a third-storey window at the school, and held him dangling by his ankles for a minute or so, before hauling him back in (Fisher).

EVERYDAY LIFE (1960S).

By the late 1960s, H.B. Beal Secondary School had more than doubled in size, which served to intimidate new students and even new teachers, and to emphasize the division between business/commerce on one side and technical subjects on the other, with the technical side itself further divided between art, shop subjects and

Home Economics. Each division still organized its students by program, which meant they had the same classmates in each subject, and frequently year after year as well, until they were through. As in the 1930s, this whole pattern resulted in social separation: commercial students did not have much to do with students in Technical or Art courses, and vice versa.

> It was sort of like we were almost in a completely separate world, encapsulated within Beal itself. ... I think there were a lot of little encapsulated groups moving around in that school (Heidenheim).

Gender divisions too were enshrined. For instance the commercial program sorted boys and girls into different specializations, while girls who wished to go into technical subjects (home economics or art), had to take grade 9 in business and commercial subjects, though boys could go straight to the shops in that grade.

On the technical side, students of this era spent a great deal of their time in shop classes made up of about fifteen students. For boys, the first year of the course involved a general introduction to a variety of areas. In the second year students took a major shop group (three related subjects) and in third and fourth year, a major subject out of those studied in year 2. Those in the five-year program devoted their last year to theory and academic subjects.

Besides the general domestic courses, female technical students had some special vocational programs open to them. Those who chose either the dietary supervisor course or the nursing assistant course spent half their time on practical subjects, and half on academics. Students in the former group spent one day a week getting practical experience in one of two local hospitals. According to the newspaper "Their boyfriends are in favour of the course too- 'They think we're going to be good housewives'"(London Free Press [LFP]. 24 Jan. 1966. Nursing assistants in training took two mornings or afternoons in a hospital each week in Grade 11; in Grade 12 it increased to three. On the wards they wore a nursing uniform, complete with cap.

> In class we studied theory and then we put into practice what we studied and learned. We took turns being patients and nurses. The student nurses would bathe their classmate patient, feed her, give her the hot water bottle, ice pack, linseed poultice, mustard plaster etc. The nurse then would become the patient another time and the patient would take the part of the nurse (Anonymous, 1982).

The teachers in all these technical courses came with a background of practical experience in their field; this was equally true of the Art department, where many of the teachers were practising artists who had not gone to any teaching institution. Aside from a requirement that they take a certain amount of drawing a week, students in the special full-time Art course could choose how to spend their day, whether it was in wandering from class to class or staying for hours in one area.

Commercial classes were twice the size of technical classes, with roughly 30 students each. In the introductory year students did data processing on key-punching machines, as well as a lot of typing and clerical practice. Students in senior courses specialized in an area such as secretarial, accounting or marketing; these classes tended to have distinct gender profiles.

In academic subjects, teachers sought to present material in ways which linked it to the students' practical experience. The actual classroom practice might vary; in general, though, teachers in these classes opened each class with an example of new work, followed by an assignment which the students then worked on for the rest of the period. Homework proved minimal.

> In staff exchanges it was sort of agreed that, you know, if you can get them to do something in class don't expect - 'cause most of them had part-time jobs - don't expect an awful lot of homework (McLagan).

From 1953, when expansion included the first school pool in the city, Beal's physical education curriculum featured swimming. Not every student enjoyed the change from more routine classroom habits. A session in the swimming pool made it a lot harder to be on time for next class; girls especially found it difficult to "get rearranged" in time (Lee). One of the older teachers had an unusual way of teaching in the pool. She would "...walk over at the edge of the pool with a stick. And if you weren't lifting your elbows, she'd whack you (Shaw)."

In addition to their time in class, students enjoyed events such as concerts, film festivals, and dances. They could participate on the yearbook staff, in one or more of the school's three bands, in a variety of school clubs and teams, or in "Martec" - the school shop - which grew out of a project by the marketing class.

Although a student was suspended from school in September 1965 for having hair which reached his collar (LFP, 7 Sept. 1965), by the last years of the decade, long hair and beards for men and "frizzy hair" and miniskirts for girls were becoming the rule.

> There were a lot of hippy types at Beal. I mean, if you didn't have hair to your shoulders, then you know, you weren't part of the crowd so to speak. It attracted that type (Shaw).

In this atmosphere, the use of marijuana and LSD became more common within school walls:

> The first floor was the entrance and the staircase. You could smell the marijuana sifting up through the... Nobody seemed to care about it, the teachers didn't do anything to stop it (Shaw).

Alcohol too featured in the challenge to traditional structures of schooling. "I had some close friends who got into drinking at school, and used to go to school drunk in Grades 11 and 12" (Shaw).

While this sort of public behaviour remained rare, other forms of challenge to authority supported it. Thus students eagerly listened to gossip and rumour that took aim at unpopular teachers. They liked to recall, for instance, how some Grade 12 boys had recently taken Mr. Fallona - the assistant to the principal, and head of the school's disciplinary structures - and dangled him out a third-storey window.

Dangling Fallona.

The story of Fallona being dangled out of a third-floor window was no doubt apocryphal - the school's version of an urban myth. Folklorists who study such myths point out that they are usually vague about the details of time and the people involved, though they can be very precise about the site. Urban myths reappear year after year, marked by both stability in certain plot elements, and variation in other (Brunvand, 1981). This is true of the Fallona myth: when former students reported the myths they always described it as having happened a few years before they entered the school, and it was always done by an anonymous group of senior boys. Indeed, some informants acknowledged the mythical quality of the story:

> The reputation I always had of Beal was that it was a tough school and there were tough people that went there. And there were lots of stories. For example I remember there was one story about how some students had taken the principal, Fallona - I don't know when he was the principal there. There was a story about how somebody had held him out of the window, upside down, banging him by his ankles sort of thing, for some reason. So there was sort of like stories like that about Beal... and the kids that went there. [...] But it was generally that kind of reputation - you know tough students. Now I never saw any evidence of that when I was actually physically there, but this was sort of always... There was a historical tinge to that, you know like it was the "old days" (Heidenheim).

Former teachers also reported hearing of the myth, but for the most part put little credence in it or, in one case, supposed it referred to an effigy (McLagan).

The popularity of the myth probably reflected the students' sense of helplessness in dealing with seemingly irrational policies on discipline. Fallona, although he mellowed considerably over the years, was always seen as being stricter (by a good measure) than his fellow teachers, whatever the decade. He seemed to appear out of nowhere, whenever students were plotting mischief. Former students consistently report that "everyone" was "terrified" or "scared to death" of Fallona (e.g. Harris, Harper, Murray, Rawson). Even fellow teachers considered him "a hard old bugger" from "the old school" (Ariss), or a "martinet" (Ritenburg).

On the other hand, like all of us, Fallona had a complex personality. Many students and teachers pointed out his belief in fairness, and his love for learning - the latter quality apparently leading to unexpected breaks in his authoritarian demeanour. At such times his other side - kind, gentle - showed through.

> The myth also draws support from the constant, latent possibility of real student retaliation. In the spring of 1953, a youth was convicted of assault, causing bodily harm for punching Fallona – and breaking his nose – in the school corridor,

Fallona spent four days in hospital; the youth was sentenced to 30 days in a more secure institution (LFP, 3 Mar. 1953; Advisory Vocational Committee, 12 Mar. 1953).

This story is clearly supported by "objective" documentary evidence - minutes of the schools advisory committee, a newspaper report, and, no doubt, court records - but it also shows interesting parallels to the window tale. One former teacher told the story this way:

> There was a lot of boys and some girls - but a lot of boys - who felt that they had been far too harshly treated. They spread the word around about how tough this man was. And there was... This is a factual occurrence. One day there was a lad who had been, I don't think he was at school at all, he had been at CCH I think and he volunteered to carry out a revenge for a boy who felt he had been unfairly treated. He came into the school and came up to the third floor. And Phil Fallona was up there for some, I don't know, regular, routine stuff. And he saw this lad and called to him and said 'you're not supposed to be up here' you see because they didn't want people in the corridors when they were disturbing the classes and so on. So the boy of course didn't know the rules and regulations and he wasn't too sure what he was.... So Phil asked him his name and he didn't recognize the name or whatever name the boy gave him. And then he asked him what class he was in. Well the boy gave him a class that didn't exist at Beal, you see. So Phil realized he was an outsider and he said 'I think you better come down with me'. I understand, I'm not sure of this, but I understand the boy did have a padlock in his hand, and he used it just like brass knuckles. He swung around and got Phil, smashed his nose down. I happended to see Phil going along the corridor, with a handkerchief, blood coming all over the place (Farmer).

The teacher concludes the narration by saying that three or four students turned in the boy, feeling that what he had done was not right. At the trial it was discovered that the youth had inherited money, so the judge ordered him to pay Fallona's expenses and lost salary (Farmer).

How much of this story is uncontested fact, and how much embellishment? Though not as common as the school window myth, other versions of this story contradict each other. One teacher even heard (and reported as true) the story this way: that a student went into Beal looking to punch Fallona with brass knuckles, instead found someone else (she thinks it was the principal) and gave him a black eye (Ritenburg).

The presence of these school myths, buried in the oral testimony of independent historical witnesses, poses a challenge to accepted techniques of oral data collection. Interview methodology has recently been subject to the same sort of fundamental critiques that have thrown light on so many areas of inquiry (Manning, 1991; Scheurich, 1992). Norman Denzin (1992) provides a summary of the positions taken by many critics:

Consider some troubling alternatives. The ethnographer's text creates the subject; subjects exist only insofar as they are brought into our written texts. Language and speech are not direct mirrors to thought, for language only distorts what it represents. Furthermore, subjects may not know what they think, change their minds, or deliberately mislead an investigation. In addition, the statements a subject offers may be influenced by other forms of textuality and interaction, including cultural standards already established, folklore, characters in novels, advertisements, and myth, as well as other filmic, literary, and scientific representations of their experiences. Flesh-and-blood individuals are copies of already reproduced cultural standards and identities. Consequently we can never get back to the flesh-and-blood individuals who live in the real world; we can only encounter their representations in our ethnographic texts.

Finally, assume that an event is inscribed multiple times on the memory disk and that each inscription is but another version of the event; hence there is no original, only multiple inscriptions (depictions, pictures and so on), each with as much validity as any other (pp. 24-5)

In these terms, then, the collection, transcription and use of oral evidence is fraught with peril.

BRINGING THE HISTORIAN BACK IN.

Memories - whether expressed as rhetoric, argument, or description - are in essence stories that people tell about themselves and their experience of reality. Left unattended the babble can be deafening. Yet if one accepts, in the words of the Popular Memory Group (1982), "that there is indeed an objective social world which has changed, historically, in ways that are potentially knowable, but does not reveal its secrets by simple observation or the testing of hypotheses" then some process of examination must proceed before we can speak with any confidence about any aspect of that objective social world. But who makes the examination? Who can claim the right to determine which version of reality prospers? Here is the crucial question. For the moment, let us clothe the historian in judicial robes.

History as a discipline has a core belief in a transcendent reality. While the study of urban myths is properly the domain of the folklorist, the removal of every fixed marker would render all history myth. The debate in history, then, focuses on the extent to which that reality can be recovered or reconstructed. While experiential approaches to historical knowledge argue that the best we can do is recover the perceptions of people from the past, more positivist approaches seek intimations of reality (Buhle and Buhle, 1988; Harlan, 1989; Spiegel, 1990; Kelly and Kelly, 1992; Stone, 1992).

Without challenging the principle that all constructed realities may have real consequences, the historian/judge seeks to disentangle the multiple meanings and messages surrounding any oral account. While an instinctive methodology might start by accepting traditional "hierarchies of credibility," Becker (1970) reminds us that the terrain of research involves not only differentiated voices but stratified voices:

> The hierarchy of credibility is a feature of society whose existence we cannot deny, even if we disagree with its injunction to believe the man at the top. When we acquire sufficient sympathy with subordinates to see things from their perspective, we know that we are flying in the face of what 'everyone knows'. The knowledge gives us pause and causes us to share, however briefly, the doubt of our colleagues (p.129).

The politicians and bureaucrats who control schools are part of a stratified system where 'those at the top have a more complete picture of what is going on than anyone else,' but oral testimony holds out hope of alternative visions. Personal memories are shaped by and within the dominant discourse - oral accounts are produced not by radically free individuals, but by individuals-in-society, and thus reflect the authorship of the situated social group (Popular Memory Group, 1982). In the end, most historians are left struggling with methods of triangulation, and establishing their own hierarchies of credibility - and those struggles go mainly unreported.

The postmodernist argument that an ethnographic account only takes meaning within a context - that description without interpretation is impossible, and all accounts are given additional layers of meaning by both writer and reader - does not disturb the historian. Rather, he or she celebrates this, and seeks to present this interpretation up front, in ways that suggest a genealogy of context surrounding the narrative of action. As Johnson and Altheide (1991) have suggested of ethnography, the authority of history "turns on the issue of context" (p. 53).

From the perspective of the historian, then, what is interesting about the Fallona myth is not so much its content, but the extent to which it illuminates the broader struggles surrounding the school. We have described elsewhere (Goodson and Dowbiggin, 1991; Anstead and Goodson, 1993a; Goodson and Anstead, 1993b) how the early history of the school involved continuous campaigns between interested groups concerned about the promises and repercussions of vocational education. Most of these battles were fought in symbolic language at the level of rhetoric. At the same time, elements in the school mediated and cooperated in the construction of the schooling experience. The teachers and administrators at LTCHS sought, in part, to turn the rhetoric and resources of vocationalism to their own ends.

It is not surprising then that in these wars, heroic and not-so-heroic myths sprang up. For the first two decades of the school's existence, its identity was bound up with that of Herbert Benson Beal, the school's founding principal. Beal's image strode the stage of local education - he was the "Great Man" personified. And it was Beal's personal goal to create in his school a "Workingman's University." From hindsight the familiar Progressive blind spots are obvious; the emphasis on pride in work and the value of labour, and the expectation that working people would have no need to go to a "real" university, all rang true in the world of social efficiency. At the same time, Beal's aggressive campaign to bring status to his school posed a challenge to the supporters of traditional academic knowledge.

By the 1970s though, the school's mythic identity had changed drastically. The school became the lightning rod for concerns over immorality and recreational drug use. To too many people in London, Beal was "Drug City." By the end of the decade, some teachers at Beal, sick of the school's reputation, engaged in a legal battle with the city's newspaper over its alleged expose of drug use at the school. But by then it was too late.

The Fallona myth takes its place somewhere on the continuum that leads from Workingman's University to Drug City. In fact, after Beal's retirement in the mid-1930s, Fallona came to be the central character in the school's historical consciousness. As principals at Beal changed more and more frequently, Fallona spent a forty-year career behind its walls. He rose to Vice-Principal in 1953 and then to a special rank as "Assistant to the Principal" for his last few years before retiring in 1969. As one teacher said: "If anybody comes to mind, when one talks about Beal, Fallona is that person, as a true character (Fry)."

COLLECTIVE MEMORY, DISSIDENT MEMORY.

The idea of a school's mythic identity is linked to oral testimonies in another way; in our interviews with students and teachers from the 1930s, we can begin to chart the emergence and maintenance of a "memory" of the school which is collectively and socially processed and constructed (Middleton and Edwards, 1990). The main themes of this sort of interpretation are: students were disciplined and showed respect for their teachers; every teacher - without exception - was good, and many went beyond the call of duty; and all students, whatever their socioeconomic background, were treated the same.

If retired teachers' or former students' stories are similar, we believe it is because they have been *collectively* constructed, negotiated and reconstructed over time. Why else would so many accounts from identical cohorts in the same school be so similar? In North America the school is one of the last socialising and collectivising public spaces. Here above all we believe *collective* memories are constructed, before being reproduced in daily discourses and subsequent shared reminiscences.

Some of the more conventional devices in the "schooldays are the happiest days" version of events are the use of positive evaluations for the main personnel in the story: "very fine gentleman", "very good student". Such rosy recollections often begin an interview as the interviewee "gives" the interviewer the expected picture and in so doing begins to explore the relationship with the interviewer. This appears clearly in the following extract from an interview with former student Fred Mitchell.

FM: I could tell you a little bit about some of them, Guy Markham was my favourite. He taught me English in first year, and history in second. I think English again in the third. He was a character, he was an ex-... he was British, and he'd served in the Canadian Army in the First World War in cavalry, Fifth Cavalry, and if you could get him going, he'd tell you a little bit about that, but he was a very sincere man. He didn't have, didn't leave his subject like some of them did, as much as some of them did - couldn't get him off what he wanted to talk about, but he made a lot of fun out of English. I can remember him, particularly when we were taking the Highwayman...but he was a very dignified man, but he'd rush out in the hall and pound on the door as "the highwayman came a riding up to the old inn door," and then rush in and recite the poem. And we were doing Shakespeare, he'd have the fellows up at the front with yardsticks fencing all across the room and telling them what they were doing wrong. This went over very well, and although he wasn't the type that you'd think, he would hold the fellows attention and there was, I think we all got a lot out of it. Different, but very effective was Ben Scott, who actually taught History and English. He was more casual and more prone to tell you what was in the headlines in the morning paper, 'cause he was a big one on current affairs, he didn't mind taking ten or fifteen minutes to talk about something that was in the paper, telling what he thought, the background, and wanting to know what you thought. He would always lead part way, get you started on something and then he would leave. And everybody knew that he was going down to the boiler room to smoke his pipe, and then he'd come back and he'd smell of tobacco, very strongly and the fellows would actually kid him about it, and he wouldn't admit it, to that's where he'd been. Effective teacher and a more of a friend with the boys then Guy Markham although they were both very fine teachers. If a fellow had problems, he might go and talk to Benny Scott about them. One of the best teachers I had there, the best at actually putting over his subject was Sanderson. He taught math.

Interestingly in only a minority of our interviews did the speaker move slowly towards a more dissident and critical view. It seemed that they were slowly feeling their way towards these views; growing to trust themselves (and their interviewers). Mitchell again provides an example of this process at work; after discussing several more teachers in a similar vein to his comments reproduced above, Mitchell turned to memories of another teacher:

He was a bully, and I don't think he was right, his personality was warped, I'll put it that way. He started every class by slamming a metre stick on the front work table because he was in the physics lab, and that was the way he'd run his class from start to finish, with a loud yelling voice. And he took no, there was no jokes, no kidding, no laughing in his class. He taught very well, 'cause you were, you were scared of him literally, because he would smack fellows on the side of the head and so on like that. I've seen him knock fellows right off their stool. But, he didn't give many detentions, he handled it all himself in his classroom, I didn't, nobody liked him. I guess he taught us, I guess we learned our subject, but it wasn't because he put it across to us in any way of a gentleman. He was a boor and a bully.

Moving from the 1930s to the 1960s, the changing nature of school mythology is matched by a crumbling of collective memory: a singular narrative no longer seems so pervasive. Take the question of drug use in the school: interviewees (both students and teachers) presented divergent memories on this issue. Several claimed that they had no memory of any drug use at the school at that time. Others were quite insistent on the opposite:

> There was a drug culture at Beal. Lot's of smoking marijuana in the halls (Shaw).

> Acid was big then, I know a lot of the kids did acid (Shaw).

> I remember during the drug scare, we had, that was in the mid '60s, late '60s, very bad, particularly marijuana and there were a few people hitting the main liner stuff, and we had visits from the Mounted Police (Ariss).

The externally-sponsored "drug city" myth, then, could draw support from the lack of an institutionally-produced collective memory.

CONCLUSIONS.

An account of everyday school life, constructed though oral testimony, offers a range of insight into the structures and practices of a particular classroom, school, or education system. As Anthony Giddens (1981; 1984; 1991), Roy Bhaskar (1979), and others have pointed out, structures are constituted by human social practices, which they themselves have shaped. Though it might be easy to see teachers and administrators as the agents whose practices reinscribed particular structures at Beal, student behaviour - passive or active - also played a role. The school's overall organization, and varying course contents, pedagogic styles and approaches to discipline all contributed to the structuration of everyday school life, as did the rules and norms of youth culture.

The process of reconstruction also uncovers empirically invalid evidence which paradoxically provides a deeper level of understanding. School-based myths and collective memories - accounts which are told and retold through time - both draw support from, and comment on, the structures implicated in that school's existence. In other words, when a historian encounters myth, the object of subsequent analysis should not be a simple debunking, but an understanding of the process which made that myth possible or even necessary.

APPENDIX: INTERVIEW SOURCES.

1930s

Teachers:

Fallona, Margaret	Morgan, Pearl

Students:

Allison, Marjorie	Brooks, Tom
Carter, Nora	Childs, Joyce*
Cushman, Russ	"M.F."
Fisher, Ben	Geddes, Irene
Hopkins, Norman	"M.K."
Kennedy, Harold	MacDonald, Evelyn
Maclaren, Hilda	Mitchell, Fred
Pruss, Glen	Spence, Gladys
Walsh, George	

* This student also took a secretarial position at LTCHS after graduating.

1960s

Teachers:

Ariss, Herbert	Farmer, Alan
Fry, Brian	Harper, Phylis
Irwin, Dennis	Jefferess, Constance
Lally, Frank	Lally, Mary Jane
Large, Robert	Leyland, Ken
McLagan, R. Evan	Murray, Hugh
Rawson, Harry	Ritenburg, Vivian

Students:

DiPietro, Carol	Harris, Doris
Heidenheim, Paul	Lee, Brenda
Shaw, Brian	

NOTES

[1] Information on the interview subjects is contained in the appendix to this paper. In this text, any direct quotation or other evidence provided by a single informant is noted by the use of a reference to that person's name without a date.

[2] A fuller version of this section can be found in Anstead and Goodson, 1993b.

REFERENCES

Advisory Vocational Committee of the Board of Education for the City of London. (1921–1972). *Minutes of the advisory vocational committee* (typescript).

Anonymous. (1982). The class of 1965. In H.B. Beal Secondary School, *Reflections, nursing assistants, 1957–1982.* London: HBBSS.

Anstead, C., & Goodson, I. (1993a). Subject status and curriculum change: Commercial education in London, Ontario, 1920–1940. *Paedagogica Historica, 29.*

Anstead, C., & Goodson, I. (1993b). Structure and mediation: Glimpses of everyday life at the London technical and commercial high school, 1920–1940. *American Journal of Education, 102.*

Becker, H. S. (1970). *Sociological work: Method and substance.* Chicago: Aldine.

Bhaskar, R. (1979). *The possibility of naturalism: A philosophical critique of the contemporary human sciences.* Harvester: Brighton.

Brunvand, J. H. (1981). *The vanishing hitchhiker: American urban legends and their meanings.* New York: Norton.

Buhl, M., & Buhl, P. (1988). The new labor history at the cultural crossroads. *Journal of American History, 75.*

Connell, R. W. (1987). *Gender and power: Society, the person, and sexual politics.* Cambridge: Polity Press.

Denzin, N. (1992). Whose Cornerville is it, anyway? *Journal of Contemporary Ethnography, 21.*

Gaffield, C. (1986). Coherence and chaos in educational historiography. *Interchange, 17.*

Giddens, A. (1981). *A contemporary critique of historical materialism.* (Vol. 1). London: Macmillan.

Giddens, A. (1984). *The constitution of society: Outline of the theory of structuration.* Cambridge: Polity Press.

Giddens, A. (1991). Structuration theory: Past, present and future. In C. G. A. Bryant & D. Jary (Eds.), *Gidden's theory of structuration: A critical appreciation.* London and New York: Routledge.

Goodson, I., & Dowbiggin, I. (1991). Vocational education and school reform: The case of the London (Canada) Technical School, 1900–1930. *History of Education Review, 20.*

Goodson, I., & Anstead, C. (1993a). *Behind the schoolhouse door: Working papers.* Toronto: Garamond.

Goodson, I., & Anstead, C. (1993b). On explaining curriculum change: H.B. Beal, organizational categories and the rhetoric of justification. *The Curriculum Journal, 4.*

H. B. Beal Secondary School. (1970). *Calendar, 1970–1971.* London: HBBSS.

Harlan, D. (1989). Intellectual history and the return of literature. *American Historical Review, 94.*

Johnson, J., & Altheide, D. (1991). Text without context and the problem of authority in Ethnographic Research. *Studies in Symbolic Interaction, 12.*

Kelly, J., & Kelly, T. (1992). Searching the dark alley: New historicism and social history. *Journal of Social History, 25.*

London Free Press (LFP). (1966, January 24).

LFP. (1953, March 3). *Advisory Vocational Committee, 12.*

LFP. (1965, September 7).

Manning, P. (1991). Strands in the postmodernist rope: Ethnographic themes. *Studies in Symbolic Interaction, 12.*

Middleton, D., & Edwards, D. (Eds.). (1990). *Collective remembering.* London, Newbury Park and New Delhi: Sage.

Popular Memory Group. (1982). Popular memory: Theory, politics, method. In R. Johnson, et al. (Eds.), *Making histories: Studies in history-writing and politics.* London: Hutchinson.

Scheurick, J. (1992). *A postmodernist review of interviewing: Dominance, resistance, and chaos.* Paper presented at the annual meeting of the American Educational Research Association, San Francisco.

Spiegel, G. (1990). History, historicism, and the social logic of the text in the middle ages. *Speculum, 65.*

Stone, L. (1992). History and Post-Modernism. *Past and Present, 135.*

"SCHOOLDAYS ARE THE HAPPIEST DAYS OF YOUR LIFE"

Ivor Goodson with Chris Anstead

> Somehow a school boy is no sooner done with his school and out in the business of life, than a soft haze of retrospect suffuses a new colour over all that he has left behind. There is a mellow sound in the tone of the school bell that he never heard in his six years of attendance.
>
> Stephen Leacock. Memories and Miseries as a School Master.

Our reflections on School memories grow out of a series of teacher life histories prepared over a sequence of research visits and meetings in the past six years. Each project used as a major source of data, intensive interviews with teachers about their working lives.

For Goodson, the critical incident came in the middle of one of his interviews with a teacher he had come to know well. The tape had just finished and he was putting a new one in. Broadly, her recall of school teaching seemed "rosy". Now retired, she looked back on a happy and harmonious professional life. As Goodson changed the tape, he teased her about it along the lines of, "hey, this all sounds great, I wish my life was as pleasant as yours has been!" Suddenly her face changed:

> Look teaching is a terrible job, its tiring, its exhausting... You fail the majority of the children and so the majority of the children fail... why would I want to talk about that...

Her interjection which was followed by more taped interviews of her fulfilling life in teaching has returned to us again and again. This is particularly the case because so many retired teachers talk in similar terms about their professional lives. School students also tend to recall their experiences of education in a similar manner.

MEMORIES OF "TECH"

In our most recent project, we have confined ourselves to the reminiscences of retired teachers and former students in one school, a pioneer technical school founded in 1916. In this way, we reduce the number of variables, and can begin to chart the emergence and maintenance of a "memory" of the school which is collectively and socially processed and constructed. Ben-Peretz has summarised some of the characteristics of retired teachers' life stories:

Retired teachers' reflection on practice, though, is not decision-orientated, nor do they seek defensible solutions to present and future problem situations. Their reflections are conclusion oriented in a highly personal manner, and serve as a summing up of the professional insights gained over time. The documented events of practising teachers are usually open-ended, not didactic, and are decision-orientated. Retired teachers seem eager to share their conclusions and insights with others. This characteristic of retired teachers' professional stories reflects Elbaz's notion of a 'community of listeners' whom the teller acknowledges and relates to. (Ben-Peretz, 1991, pp 17-18)

Our recall of that "interjection of dissent' however makes us unhappy with any monolithic judgement, whether about retired teachers' or former students' stories. If they are similar, we believe it is because they have been *collectively* constructed, negotiated and reconstructed over time. Why else would so many accounts from identical cohorts in the same school be so similar? In North America the school is one of the last socialising and collectivising public spaces. Here above all we believe *collective* memories are constructed.

Yet, in our interviews, although a broadly agreed collective memory can be readily tapped, a second sort of memory exists on the margins. In his research notes, Anstead reflected on these two responses from previous students of "Tech", our case study secondary institution. One type of interview is that which characterises school as a happy experience.

In these interviews, the subject stays on topic, answers questions in useful ways, and provides a lot of information to add to our brick by brick reconstruction of 'Tech'. In this sort of interview, the schooling experience is invariably presented in rosy tones. Frequently comparison to the present system of education is made, with many negative comments about the latter. The main themes of this sort of interpretation are: students were disciplined and showed respect for their teachers; every teacher - without exception - was good, and many went beyond the call of duty; and all students, whatever their socioeconomic background, were treated the same. The positive view of their school days probably results partly from the selection process; those people who most enjoyed or valued their school experience were most likely to answer our ad. Yet, I would not want to dismiss the positive out of hand; there is probably some truth behind the platitudes.

But another type of memory can also be tapped among a minority of former school members.

A few former students present more critical or analytical views of their past. Two such interviews took place last week. These students still have a generally positive view of 'Tech.', and present their school days as the 'best of times'. Yet they are also willing to say that certain teachers were not very good (or even unbalanced in one case). They can point to some types of discrimination, either in the school, or on the part of outsiders describing the school.

The most common memory of schooling often has a rather rehearsed feel to it as if the speaker knows he or she is telling you something you expect to hear. It could be a "collective school memory" into which the inmates of the school have seen socialised and which they have engaged in reproducing in their daily discourses and subsequent shared reminiscences.

Becker's notion of the hierarchy of credibility partially explains how the "reality" of the school is produced by participants, with those in power having a disproportionate influence on reality definition. The collective memory, "what everybody knows" about school is partly a testimony to the power of "the critical reality definers" within the school community:

> We can use the notion of a *hierarchy of credibility* to understand this phenomenon. In any system of ranked groups, participants take it as given that members of the highest group have the right to define the way things really are. In any organization, no matter what the rest of the organization chart shows, the arrows indicating the flow of information point up, thus demonstrating (at least formally) that those at the top have access to a more complete picture of what is going on than anyone else. Members of lower groups will have incomplete information, and their view of reality will be partial and distorted in consequence. Therefore, from the point of view of a well socialized participant in the system, any tale told by those at the top intrinsically deserves to be regarded as the most credible account obtainable of the organizations' workings. And since, as Summer pointed out, matters of rank and status are contained in the mores, this belief has a moral quality. We are, if we are proper members of the group, morally bound to accept the definition imposed on reality by a superordinate group in preference to the definitions espoused by subordinates. (By analogy, the same argument holds for the social classes of a community.) Thus, credibility and the right to be heard are differentially distributed through the ranks of the system. (Becker, 1970, pp. 126-128)

Thus:

> The hierarchy of credibility is a feature of society whose existence we cannot deny, even if we disagree with its injunction to believe the man at the top. When we acquire sufficient sympathy with subordinates to see things from their perspective, we know that we are flying in the face of what 'everyone knows'. The knowledge gives us pause and causes us to share, however briefly, the doubt of our colleagues. (1970, p. 129)

As well as the power of critical reality definers in establishing a collective memory, the rehearsed quality of "traditional" school memories is partly a response to the interview situation. Interviewees commonly seek to provide a coherent account drawing on their pre-interview stories — the way they have told the stories of their lives to themselves and to previous listeners.

> ...the subject attempts to create a consistent and coherent story for the interviewer's benefit — even going to the extent of rehearsing it prior to the interview. It is indeed odd how, sometimes, respondents are able to repeat more or less in the same words a story told two months earlier — as if they had rehearsed and learnt a script. Of relevance here are all those features which psychologists have designated 'demand characteristics'; the respondent enters the situation, tries to work out what the interviewer is getting at, and proceeds to answer in accord with this. (Plummer, 1983, p. 102)

Some of the more conventional devices in the "schooldays are the happiest days" version of events are the use of positive evaluations for the main personnel in the story: "very fine gentleman", "very good student". Such rosy recollections often begin an interview as the interviewee "gives" the interviewer the expected picture and in so doing begins to explore the relationship with the interviewer. For instance:

> I really don't have all that much to tell you other then that I did go there and it was Tech. That's the only name people called it in those days. You know, you go to Tech. Our, I think he was our classroom teacher, but it was a Mr. Oates. O-a-t-e-s. And he taught shorthand, and writing. He was a marvellous writer. Gee, you should see what he put up on the board, it was great. And Mr. Squire was our typing teacher and that was really good. You'd have a roomful of girls, oh we did have one boy too I think. But anyway, you go in at 1:30 and you'd hear click, click, click, click, click. Everybody'd be sitting there, and he was very good, and we typed to music. (Margaret Allison Interview, February 20, 1992, p.1)

Or take the following introductory statement from two former pupils of "Tech School", Nora Carter and Glen Pruss.

NC: Near as I can figure it out ... I started ... I went to kindergarten in 1928 and then to public school to I think 1929, and I went to Beck for two years and then I went to Special Art at Beal Tech. And at that time Mrs. Maudie Cryderman, have you ever heard of her? Wonderful human being, just, I just thought she was the greatest thing that ever was and she was a fine artist. And we had quite a big class, and I don't remember a lot of names from that period, you know, it's a long time ago. And she was my headroom, home-room teacher during the years that I was there, and of course I took the other courses like sewing and drafting, and the things that, take to, fine arts. And Mr. Robertson was the principal of the school, a very fine gentleman.

GP: He was the technical side.

NC: Yes, and I couldn't remember his first name. Wasn't Mr. Beal there?

GP: No, no.

NC: He was when I was there. I'm sure.

GP: When I went there it was Robertson and, I never went to the Commercial side I guess.

NC: I don't remember that.

CA: Well, we have that all on the records anyway so we can find that out.

NC: And, I think it was a very wonderful school to go to at that time. Certainly, I don't know about now, of course it's all changed. I did go back to a reunion once, and I, the school had been built on it, and I wandered through halls and it wasn't very familiar to me. And I didn't see *anyone* I knew. That would be in the, it was after I came home from England, after the War. So it's probably in the early 50s when I went to a reunion. As I said, I didn't see anyone I knew, or anyone that evoked any memories. And I, detail, the sort of detail that you want perhaps will come out in the questions that you ask. And as I say he does, he was a very good student and, never missed a day, and got medals or something for it. So, perhaps he'll be more interesting then I will be to talk to.

In these early exchanges, the school is unproblematically "a very wonderful school". Later on in the interview though, the two interviewees began to talk to each other and to provoke a far more complex memory of the school. This we might call the "dissident memory" where the "truth" begins to deviate from the version of events that is conventionally accepted, worked for and normally recounted.

NC: What was the teacher's name who taught English who was so addicted to aspirin? We were talking about him. And he taught, well we took English.

GP: Yeah.

NC: I took the courses that were required. He was at tech.

GP: Yeah.

NC: MacIntyre?

GP: No. I was thinking about him last night.

CA: What was his problem?

NC: He was a highly nervous man, and he was a wonderful teacher, I even enjoyed Shakespeare with him, and since my son later became a Shakespearean actor, I had to learn a little bit more about it. But we did the *Taming of the Shrew*, and *Merchant of Venice*. And he would make us take parts and he, but he raced up and down the aisles and, he was very dramatic. And he was highly nervous and he sent my brother, or one of us over to the corner drugstore, it was a Mr. Allen, on the corner of Maitland was it?

GP: No, Colburne, no Waterloo...

NC: No, no. Maitland? William, no?

GP: William Street.

NC: There was a drugstore right on the corner, I can see it plain as plain with the curved glass in the windows, the door, a very fancy sort of Victorian Door that went in. And he'd send us there for aspirin tablets. And he'd just take, he'd dump a few out in his hand, I think he chewed them.

GP: Mr. McFadden.

NC: McFadden. And, *oh* he was a wonderful English teacher. He really challenged you, and brought the best out in you. And everybody seemed to like him. I think we enjoyed him because it was like going to a play.

CA: [laughs] Were there any teachers that weren't so good that had...?

NC: Oh, the one who [laughs] I didn't know him because he was on the commercial side, but who had the detention class, was a real... *Oh*, he was a, well.

CA: Was that Walker?

NC: Martinet, you know just, tall blond man.

GP: I can remember the Fallonas. Mr. Fallona and his sister.

NC: Yes.

GP: They were Italian. They were something else.

CA: What do you mean?

GP: Well, they, you marched to their tune, don't go left when you should have went right. Just didn't get, and then we had a Mr O'Donell. From Dublin.

NC: Irish as Paddy's pig.

GP: And he taught French.

NC: [laughs]

GP: I had a spare, so they sent me, they were going to, but you couldn't understand him when he spoke the King's English, let alone Irish. So him and I got into an argument one day, so he put me in the hallway, and I thought "I'm not putting up with this", so I went right up stairs to the office to the Principal. And next thing you know, this Mr. O'Donell is standing looking through the door, so the Principal calls him in and he said, "Mr. Pruss will not be in your class any longer".

[laughter]

GP: He said, "what's your problem?" I said "well you can't understand the man when he talks the King's English, so how do you understand an Irishman from Dublin, teaching you French?"

[laughter]

GP: I said "it sounds like something from some other foreign country". I said "I just don't get along with him, you leave me in there, why I'll just be in a problem all the time with him". So the rest of them, they caught on, so there's a lot of them got out of the class doing the same thing. Get in an argument with him, and then get out of it.

NC: What did Mr. Thomas, "Trombone" Thomas teach?

GP: He taught, labwork. And we knew we had a squealer in the class. So this day, some of them got in ahead and they went up and got a piece of phosphorus out of the water, and they put it in this kid's desk. [laughs] We called him "Trombone" because he was in the orchestra and he played the trombone.

NC: That was a teacher.

GP: Yeah, and he [laughs] comes whistling and this kid's sitting there and all of a sudden the smoke started coming out of his desk. So he took the kid out in the hall and punished him. But we did it because this kid was squealing on us.

NC: Did you know that he was the...?

GP: Yeah, we found out that he was telling, we got in the classroom ahead of Mr. Thomas, and if anything went on, why this kid would tell him afterwards. We thought "well we'll cool your heels for you".

CA: Did you get away with a lot of that sort of borderline stuff?

NC: It was kind of, it was a more relaxed [laughs] atmosphere then Sir Adam Beck, believe me. But, we used to smoke in the boiler room. In those days, you know, it was just, girls were just beginning to smoke and that sort of thing. And the man who was in charge of the boiler room, he was *very* understanding, he let us smoke in there sometimes.

CA: And did the teachers just sort of look the other way?

NC: No, if they caught you, you were in trouble. It was forbidden of course to smoke on the school grounds even. But they were good years and I remember them with, a lot of nostalgia. I just wish I'd paid more attention to things then, then I did.

Interestingly in a number of our interviews, the speaker would move slowly towards the more dissident and critical views. It often seems that they are slowly feeling their way towards these views; growing to trust themselves (and maybe their interviewers). Initially, they adopt the positive views which have been collectively constructed and reaffirmed but as they get into their stride, more and more their individual experience and voice takes over. Fred Mitchell provides a good example of this process at work:

FM: I could tell you a little bit about some of them, Guy Markham was my favourite. He taught me English in first year, and history in second. I think English again in the third. He was a character, he was an ex, he was British, and he'd served in the Canadian Army in the First World War in cavalry, Fifth Cavalry, and if you could get him going, he'd tell you a little bit about that, but he was a very sincere man. He didn't have, didn't leave his subject like some of them did, as much as some of them did - couldn't get him off what he wanted to talk about, but he made a lot of fun out of English. I can remember him, particularly when we were taking the Highwayman...but he was a very dignified man, but he'd rush out in the hall and pound on the door as "the highwayman came a riding up to the old inn door," and then rush in and recite the poem. And we were doing Shakespeare, he'd have the fellows up at the front with yardsticks fencing all across the room and telling them what they were doing wrong. This went over very well, and although he wasn't the type that you'd think, he would hold the fellows attention and there was, I think we all got a lot out of it. Different, but very effective was Ben Scott, who actually taught History and English. He was more casual and more prone to tell you what was in the headlines in the morning paper, 'cause he was a big one on current affairs, he didn't mind taking ten or fifteen minutes to talk about something that was in the paper, telling what he thought, the background, and wanting to know what you thought. He would always lead part way, get you started on something and then he would leave. And everybody knew that he was going down to the boiler room to smoke his pipe, and then he'd come back and he'd smell of tobacco, very strongly and the fellows would actually kid him about it, and he wouldn't admit it, to that's where he'd been. Effective teacher and a more of a friend with the boys then Guy Markham although they were both very fine teachers. If a fellow had problems, he might go and talk to Benny Scott about them. One of the best teachers I had there, the best at actually putting over his subject was Sanderson. He taught math. The math course was different than the collegiate's have. We had a book for, I believe it was called *Mathematics for Technical Schools* and it was more geared to what we'd need in trade afterwards. And also, it was a sort of a mixture of math, I don't think we had a subject like the collegiate had, of geometry, trigonometry, and algebra. It was more combined, like part of the year you take algebra, and then change over. And when we had trig., many of the problems were actually surveying problems and similar to that. I don't think we reached the level of the collegiate in any of them. Afterwards I had to, I went...because I quit in the middle of my fourth year, I had to go back, later when I was in the navy I took some of my math by correspondence school and I got my grade twelve that way. Of course it was fourth year. The drafting teachers were Bessant for mechanical in the senior years, Moodie was, taught grade nine, first year. I was not in that, I was in the math and I had Brown, who was also the architectural drafting teacher in my first year. So the two that I had were Bessant for mechanical and Brown for architectural. They were both little short men, about 5 foot 5, rather round, Bessant was a more cheerful person than Brown. Both very well liked, strict but not overbearing, Bessant was very knowledgeable in his subject and we all liked him. Brown was, more sedate, a good man in his field, I never was close to him as I was to Bessant. But he was okay. One of the quirks he had was, across the road was a funeral home, and every time there was a funeral when the casket was coming out, he would make his way over to the window, stand with his hands behind his back and go up and down on his toes and watch the casket come out. I don't know, he just did that every day, because there was always a funeral. I, the subject...they both presented their subject well and I received a pretty good grounding in drafting from them.

Mitchell then turned to memories of a specific teacher:

He was a bully, and I don't think he was right, his personality was warped, I'll put it that way. He started every class by slamming a metre stick on the front work table because he was in the physics lab, and that was the way he'd run his class from start to finish, with a loud yelling voice. And he took no, there was no jokes, no kidding, no laughing in his class. He taught very well, 'cause you were, you were scared of him literally, because he would smack fellows on the side of the head and so on like that. I've seen him knock fellows right off their stool. But, he didn't give many detentions, he handled it all himself in his classroom, I didn't, nobody liked him. I guess he taught us, I guess we learned our subject, but it wasn't because he put it across to us in any way of a gentleman. He was a boor and a bully.

Collective Memory, Dissident Memory

The interviews with Nora and Glen and with Fred Mitchell capture in fascinating juxtaposition the existence of both the mainstream *collective memory* and a more iconoclastic *dissident memory*. It is worth speculating on why these two memories often exist at the same time and are only slowly uncovered and exposed.

It is, we think, important to remember schools are set up as socialising and collectivising public spaces; socialising goes on through daily work in classrooms and staffrooms. Schools deliberately construct as part of their daily business 'collective memories' and teachers and students are themselves socialised into these memories throughout their school lives. The collective memory socialises the 'situated self' of the teacher and student in the school. For the teacher, the dominant collective memory, then, is part of the situated knowledge of the workplace, part of the situated self.

The institutional construction of collective memory seeks to overlay the individuals' memory with a meta-narrative of selective images and realities.

> The notion of *institutional remembering and forgetting* is not simply a reference to the fact that social organizations create records in the form of minutes, archives and financial audits, but also refers to the large-scale manipulation of what should or could be remembered - socially organized remembering and forgetting. (Middleton & Edwards, 1990, p. 10)

Schools are past masters of this construction of collective memory

> The morning recitation of the Pledge of Allegiance in American schools exemplifies both the joint and commemorative nature of the *social foundation and context of individual memory*. The unison of voices provides an environment of collectively realized performance within which the novice can bridge any gaps of individual incompetence. At the same time each re-performance consolidates the authority of this commemorative practice, and the authority of those who obligate the children's performance. However, even the catechisms and ceremonies of ritual commemoration are the product of conversation and argument, as people have discussed how an event might best be commemorated, what precisely should be said and done and how it might be realized on each occasion.(Middleton & Edwards, 1990, p. 8 - 9)

But few sociologists or psychologists would take the view that the 'situated self' comprises the total self. A good deal of literature exists that there is for teachers, as for others, a 'substantial self' which precedes involvement in teaching and which clearly surfaces when teaching is over.

the substantial self, and the values it incorporates, is itself socially conditioned, especially by early and powerful significant others and social groups (generalized others). The assumptions we learn to make about ourselves and our worlds become embedded in generalized perspectives and the correctness and accuracy of these are in turn confirmed by contact with people who have similar perspectives ('reference groups'). So, when we enter the world of work (or any similar new arena) we open ourselves to a potential conflict - between the beliefs and values built up in our early years and sustained by our significant and generalized others and those exemplified by the people with whom we now interact every day. (Nias, 1989, p.43)

In the memories of older people, elderly ex-students or retired teachers, it could be argued the substantial self re-emerges strongly to sponsor and to prompt the 'dissident memory'.

that part of the self which is relatively free of social constraints: it is impulsive and capable of inventing new ideas or meanings not sent in by the 'other'. It is that most private core of inner experience which has a degree of autonomy ... The 'me' cannot be anything but conformist ... [but when we realize] that in some respect we acted against the grain of society, such a realisation is awareness of the 'I' and its capacities. (Open University: Introduction to Sociology Course Team, D207 (1981) *Self in Social Context*, Milton Keynes: Open University, quoted in Nias, 1989, p .23)

The old conflict between what the school collective memory tells people 'everyone knows' and the private experiences which constantly throw up contradictions and ambiguities emerges. In the situated and collectivised atmosphere of the school these disjunctures are held in suspension. (We have at this point a possibly different version of the self - the *suspended* self). Upon retirement this suspension of ambiguity and contradiction is no longer a daily necessity. The collective and dissident memories can sometimes be discerned side by side.

Hence the great value of the school memories is that they allow the suppressed tension between "what everybody knows" about schooling and what people have actually experienced to re-emerge. The price of living and working in an institution is often that we have to suppress our own definitions of the situation for the functions of the greater collective enterprise. The development of life histories builds on this tension between formal functionalist, official definitions of what everyone knows; the collective memory and inner definition, the dissident memory:

In the adequate life history we must constantly keep in mind the situation both as defined by others and by the subject; such a history will not only define both versions of the situation but let us see clearly the pressure of the formal situation and the force of the inner private definition of the situation. One of the acutest needs in cultural theory is to specify the series of situations through which the average organism in the culture must come; this specification will probably turn out to be a more specific view of the culture patterns, a view of culture as it is actually experienced by emerging members of the group.

The usual error in regard to this criterion is to count only with the formal social situation and to overvalue it by assuming that all persons come into the formally defined situation with the same experience and define it in the same way. Only "normal" persons are able to do this. The mistake of overvaluing the existing situation is the sociological error *par excellence*. (Dollard, 1949, pp. 32-33)

We hope that by pursuing life histories and broadly-conceived teacher memories, we can avoid the sociological error par excellence and move to a situation where the teacher's memories are sociologically located and valued. What is clear is that for too long scholars have been assembling detailed accounts of schools without consulting those people who have spent a lifetime at the centre of action.

REFERENCES

Becker, H. S. (1970). *Sociological work: Method and substance.* Chicago: Aldine.

Ben-Peretz, M. (1991, September). *Scenes from the past: Retired teachers remember.* Paper presented at the 5th ISATT Conference, University of Surrey, Guilford.

Middleton, D., & Edwards, D. (Eds.). (1990). *Collective remembering.* London, Newbury Park and New Delhi: Sage.

Nias, J. (1989). *Primary teachers talking: A study of teaching as work.* London and New York: Routledge.

Plummer, K. (1983). *Documents of life: An introduction to the problems and literature of a humanistic method.* London: George Allen & Unwin.

LIFE HISTORIES AND PROFESSIONAL PRACTICE: DATA IN PROCESS

Ivor Goodson

I sometimes think that, like cigarettes, life histories should come with a warning. Not so much, 'smoking can seriously damage your health', more 'life histories can seriously impair your understanding'. This is because life histories are such complex and often contradictory mechanisms. Much has to do with their location: they exist at the intersections and on the sites of our multi-faceted struggles for selfhood and identity. By their very location, then, they are supremely suited to provide windows into the complexities of our social being. Life histories then, must be treated with great care, but the reward for social inquiry can, nonetheless, be great.

Let me mention one or two contradictions that hint at the difficulties. In the current period of post-modern fragmentation, with traditions and established practices coming under great threat, our struggles for identity face remarkably chaotic and disparate environments. The life history may serve in the face of a fragmentary existence as a site to re-establish some sense of unity and coherence. The more fragmentary our existence, then, the more unified our life stories may become. At this point, our life experience and our story of it may be almost oppositional. This relationship between life experience and life story will, I suspect, oscillate and alter during the life course, and at different historical times.

Likewise, the social script of expectations, which each of us comes into the world with, create different 'parts' for different people. For the rich white male, the social script written before birth, (shall we say when 'his name is put down for Eton'), may prove acceptable and will be lived and storied as planned. For those of other class, race and gender, the script that is written by society will be more oppressive and the life may be lived as an attempt to deconstruct the social script.

Life stories then, to repeat, are contradictory mechanisms. For this reason, among others, we have developed a distinction between life stories and life histories. This does not resolve many of these issues, but seeks to wrestle with some of the factors at play. The life story is the story we narrate about the events of our lives. This story often refers mostly to the inner dialogue which I have called, 'our reflexive project of selves'.

The life history is collaboratively constructed by a life storyteller and life story interviewer/researcher. Therein, the aspiration is different to that of the life story. The aim is to 'locate' the life story as it operates in particular historical circumstances. A range of data is employed: documents, interviews with relevant others, theories, texts, even physical locations and buildings. This data is, so-to-speak, 'triangulated' to locate the life story as a social phenomenon existing in historical time. The life history then, aims to create a different story to that of the personal life story. In this story, the wider worlds of power and meaning are situations in which the life story is embedded. Without this, we argue the life story is a limited perspective and a potentially dangerous data site, for as Samuel has argued: "History from below .... without some larger framework ... becomes a cul-de-sac and loses its subversive potential" (Samuel, 1989, p.23).

Developing life history data can help in broadening our understanding of the teacher's professional work. The following section provides one example of how this pursuit of research data comprising the teachers' whole life perspective on their work and practice can transform our understandings. Not all such data provides such smooth transformation as in this example; in some ways it all seems 'too neat'. But this example has been chosen precisely because it does show the power of life history work with unusual clarity. In the concluding section, the importance of such work is assessed and its potential for our work on professional practices tentatively determined.

INTRODUCING COMPUTERS INTO A TEACHERS LIFE

In the period of the late 1980's and early 1990's, the province of Ontario went through a massive programme of investment to provide computers in school classrooms. A number of research projects were funded to examine and evaluate this initiative. In the years 1990 to now, we have been working on one of the largest projects and subsequently analysing and writing up the data for a new book called, 'Computer Wars' (Goodson and Lanksheer, 1999).

The project team comprised a large group of research fellows and faculty members covering a spectrum from the techno-fanatical to the Luddite-cynic. In this chapter we examine one teacher's response to computers being introduced into his classroom and in doing so we comment on the methodological nuances of our research study.

In the initial period of our research we focused mainly on classroom observation and on technological orientation workshops. However, Goodson the project coordinator and Mangan the senior research officer were concerned to broaden the focus away from an analysis of technological implementation. Goodson a non-technical Luddite and Mangan a techno-enthusiast with sociological reservations began to argue for a set of life history studies to search for a broader set of insights into the impact of computers on the teacher's life and work.

In this chapter we focus on one teacher to show how this broader focus pushed to reformulate our initial 'representations' of a teacher's response to computers. Our first data on Jim, a geography teacher, focuses on his response to being invited to join the project and to the early orientation meeting.

MM: Um...so it wasn't explained to you how they happened to pick you or uh, why they landed on you rather than someone else in the department?

Jim: No, I was just stopped - stopped in the hall by the principal and PN. I didn't know PN ahead of time, so... and it sounded good at the time, but I regretted after that I had done it, OK? Although I have some... non-regrets, too, because now I know a little bit about it, and I'm going to become involved, and I slacked off, mainly because - not mainly because - my department head [DS] is so involved in computers, so - and he got involved, so he took up the slack for me and he'll have to re-teach me a lot of it.

MM: So, did you understand that the project would require a fair bit of in-service training when you first got involved?

Jim: Oh, yes, yes, yes. I - I've had a sinking feeling that this was going to happen. But, uh, I went to the first number of meetings, but it did fall off after, OK?, and it's - I must admit totally fallen off right now. So, I'm gonna have to pull myself up by the bootstraps and start again next fall.

Jim then from the beginning struck a note of reservation 'that sinking feeling' which could sometimes express itself as 'resistance'.

MM: That's interesting, 'cause one of the other teachers recently said they found that meeting a little intimidating with all those honchos there, and uh, but you didn't feel that way about it?

Jim: No, no. I try not to let people intimidate me... [MM laughs]... if at all possible. I was there as a volunteer, I wasn't being paid. They wouldn't - there's no threat on my life - I mean, they're not gonna cut me off or anything. So they can say, 'You're doing a crappy job.' That's fine, OK, uh... Give me a pat on the back, but it's not gonna change my salary, it's not gonna change my position, it's you know, I'm the one involved, so, you know, I don't find people intimidating me or [phone is ringing].

Our response to Jim on the research team was not unlike the way in which teachers come to stereotype and sort out the children in their class on the first few days. Working with lots of people you tend to create shorthand categories and stereotypes - they are inadequate, and you know that but they can become ossified. 'First impressions stick'.

One first impression of Jim was that he was a 'resister'. Knowing Goodson's Luddite predilections the research team kept noting, 'we think we've found you a resister'. 'Hey Jims the Luddite you've been looking for'. Although these were jokes they expressed serious aspects of the truth - Goodson did have reservations about computers and seeing a teacher express these through his reservations and resistances confirmed their feelings. Sometimes Jim expressed this quite directly.

MM: Yeah. Well, I guess where that might tie back in with computer use is...one thing that some teachers express concern about is that using computers is a equalizing and unif...an imposition of a more uniform curriculum. In other words, you can't alter the computer curriculum to the same extent that you could play around with your own lesson plans and your own teaching materials and so forth. Do you see that as a danger in any way? Or?...

Jim: No, because...not in my life time. The computer isn't going to take my place.

MM: No?

Jim: No way.

MM: You don't think it will limit your freedom either though?

Jim: It'll... it'll limit your freedom if you become a slave to it and enter...everything centres around the computer, then, yes, your freedom is gone. But as far as I'm concerned, my lack of using it, is pretty indicative right now that maybe I'm not going to let somebody else...something else interfere with me. No, I've always thought of it as a super supplement to other things that go on in the classroom, other types of lessons. Okay, to build up a basis of kids being able to use it for the lab work. Where they're on their own and they have to interpret or maybe they have to draw or they have to extrapolate something. Because I want to get back to the spreadsheet. It looks so neat. So I did a lot of work on that. It's not going to take my place. At least, not in seven years, okay.

At other times he expressed a more ambivalent view - seeing the problems for his own work life and then focusing on the rationale from the point of view of his students.

VR: Uh...You said that the teaching aids and AV material and things like that have changed. How do you feel computers fit in to that?

Jim: Well, it's the next change that I've got to swallow. As I've admitted to you before, I'm still kind of frightened of it because I haven't gotten into the swing of it yet. And it's going to start very soon and I'm crossing my fingers that I'm not going to fall on my face. If I fall in my face I'm still going to live, so I'm not going to worry about it. But it's absolutely so useful a tool that it's gotta come, and I've gotta just break my back and get away from maybe old-fashioned things that I have been doing and get on with the new because uh...all the kids coming out of high school should have some degree of expertise in computers. And I'm not going to preach about Geography being so important that it's absolutely necessary but just the application of computers for a lot of jobs, for the simple reason that Geography is not going to be something they're are going to be working with for the rest of their lives.

From our point of view then Jim was a resister who expressed some ambivalence. In his actions though Jim was clear - again and again and again from early 1989 he was 'just too busy' to actually introduce computers into his classroom or go to the computer laboratory with his class. He said he was 'frightened' of falling 'on my face' and his actions confirmed this. But he promised that in the summer of 1989 he would buy his own computer and develop some 'stuff' for his class. In the event he did nothing and on field notes confirm the growing conviction that Jim was not going to 'buy in' to computer.

Jim didn't seem particularly thrilled to see us. Despite his avowals at the end of last term, he quickly confessed that he had spent his entire summer either at the cottage or travelling in Eastern Canada. No mention of summer computer projects. I told him that I was now the Geography P.I., and that as such, I would be willing to help him sort out some applications for his classes. He indicated that he would try to develop some stuff soon, with the help of Steve and myself. However, he would be coaching soccer again this year, and he would be absent the third week of September, on a tour of Northern Ontario sponsored by the Ontario Mining Association.

Similar to last year, Jim already has a lot of 'extra' things scheduled for this year. He said that he was one of a group of teachers selected to attend a week-long session on Mining in Ontario, to be held in northern Ontario from Sept. 23-30. This means that he will be missing an entire week of school already, and his class will have a substitute teacher. In addition to this, he will still be coaching junior boys' soccer this year. He said he didn't plan to, but after finishing in first place last year, he just couldn't say no!

Or in the summer of 1990:

We now seem to have established good rapport with almost everyone in the project. Jim may be the one exception. He seems wary of us, although I think he likes us personally. The other day, at the Brock Art show, he commented that, "I avoid everything to do with computers". Nothing ruins a relationship like guilt, and I think he feels guilty around us. He feels he has not fulfilled some obligation he made to the project, and to us as part of that project. Even so, he always seems friendly towards us personally.

If for the research team Jim was 'our resister' to his colleagues Jim was a 'beached whale', 'a burnt out case' - clapped out and ready to retire. They very directly expressed the belief that Jim would 'never' take up computers.

Steve then turned to me with what he called a 'simple question'. He wanted to know what was going to happen to Geography in the project. Jim hasn't used the lab yet, and as far as Steve is concerned, is never going to use it. He said that he will tell us that he is going to use it, but he'll come up with excuse after excuse and never use it. He knows, because he's been through it with him before, with no success. He is concerned that Jim will be representing all geographers in our reports. I assured him that that would not be so, but he felt uncomfortable with the situation. He said that he didn't want to push us into anything, but it might be a good idea to visit his classes as well. I told him what Jim told us of his plans for this year, but that he has just been too busy so far. He said that it was true, but Jim will always be too busy with other things to find time to use the computer.

There were people in geography that were already involved in dealing with computers but not on this level. Not on a level where we can actually teach kids using the computers, because they don't have them. And this was an opportunity to actually have enough computers to really use them in the classroom. So I wanted geography involved. It didn't have to be me particularly. But I'd already tried to get Jim involved with the Commodore and I mean, I'm not talking about a one-shot try. We tried over and over, every P.D. day we had there for a while, we had at least something involving, you know, getting them hands-on a computer. And nothing happened and I knew that that was likely to happen again.

Both the research team and the other geography teacher came ultimately to agree that Jim was 'representative' of a type.

MM: Yeah, well it's, I mean for one thing we did want the project to be an effort in moving into some new areas like, you say, not just science, math, and accounting. So that was one of the reasons we wanted to have geography and some of the other subjects. And actually whatever the history behind it, I'm sort of glad that we've got Jim because I think one of the things that happens too often in these evaluation projects is that you only get really enthusiastic and sometimes people with a great deal of background knowledge, as your own.

Steve: Yes that's right.

MM: And it creates a sort of artificial situation. I mean, one thing that I think is going to be useful to our evaluation is to try to figure out what the sort of sources of resistance or reluctance for people like Jim are. Because I don't think that you can expect everybody to embrace computer use in schools with open arms.

Steve: Nope. He certainly proved that. No, I agree. As a research tool you've to look at the whole spectrum and he's certainly part of that spectrum. There is no question about it. But at the same time if you were going to, you know, once you'd established that, there is an awful lot of information that came out of things that somebody who is **using** the computers could provide that he'll never be able to provide you with.

MM: Right. Which is exactly why we wanted to get you more involved.

So by now the researchers and Jims colleagues had more or less come to a consensual on Jim. In the field notes it was expressed this way.

Although I do not want to attempt psychoanalysis of Jim, the following factors seem to me to combine to account for his reluctance to get involved with computers:

- personal insecurity: habits of methodical preparation; fear of being unable to completely master or control the material during a classroom presentation; inability to completely control the material presented by the programs.

- established teaching patterns: related to above, his presentations seem very uniform, semester to semester. He has chosen certain teaching aids which he has used for up to twenty years without change. 'Socratic' style.

- personal relationship with students: Jim likes to get to know them personally; he jokes a lot with them, makes individual eye contact in every class; acts quite fatherly towards most of them.

- individualized treatment: Jim has repeatedly affirmed his disinterest in marking programs, because he feels there are intangible considerations which must go into a student's final grade. He feels computers are too insensitive to the individual needs and circumstances of each student.

- technophobia: and finally, Jim has repeatedly described himself as 'old-fashioned', by which he means not only that he uses old-fashioned teaching techniques, but that he is committed to a traditional concept of literacy. He emphasizes the need to be able to write well, and to deal with maps and written material. He may be suspicious that computers undermine that traditional literature culture.

And there probably matters would have stayed. However, by now we had undertaken and were transcribing Jim's life history interviews. These life history collaborations allowed us to see events in a crucially different way from more normal research observations and interviews. They provide 'grounded conversations' to deeply explore issues. Some of the burnt-out case hypothesis was actually brought up in these interviews.

MM: I should probably know this from earlier interviews but it's slipped my mind. How close to retirement are you?

Jim: Seven years.

MM: Seven years.
Jim: Well, five to seven years.
MM: So it's not just around the corner.
Jim: No.
MM: Because I mean, what I'm getting at there is I wonder whether...I mean even from...if it were me I think I might wonder about whether the investment in learning something as complex and as big as Computer Assisted Learning at this stage was going to pay off for me...in the few remaining years of my career. Do you think that's part of it, at all?
Jim: No.
MM: No? You are still interested in new...
Jim: Seven years would be my 90 factor, okay. If I was totally fed-up or ill or something with the other..age 55...with penalty or it could go on a little bit longer. So...no, in terms of a fiscal investment I don't think so. I can't say my wife and I are poor, so it's not that.

Other matters emerged in the interviews. As well as turning 50 Jim's dad had just died and he was spending a lot of time visiting his ill mother.

VR: And do your parents still live in Windsor?
Jim: Uh..no my uh..(long pause)..my father died about four years ago and my mother is in a nursing home right now.
VR: Nearby?

Jim: No, down by Blythe, not too far. It's only an hour and 15 minutes away. So I see her, but uh..to tell you personally she's not in very good shape, right now, so...

VR: It makes it difficult.

Jim: Uh...We're expecting it, you know, her to die, okay, we all know what's happening and uh.. she wants it that way so...

Hence, we began to get some sense of the way the trajectory of the project 'collided' with the trajectory of Jim's life. An alternative hypothesis was thereby generated. Maybe Jim was telling the truth when he said, as he kept saying: "I'll get to it in the end". This did seem after all a tough time in his life: burying his Dad, immersed in his mothers' final illness, turning 50. At another level we begun to view it as almost heroic that he would even attempt a major new undertaking under such circumstances - Jim's acceptance of all the blame seemed suddenly stoic.

MM: I know you've got to go soon. Do you have any other comments about how the project's gone? Do you feel like you've gotten enough support from us at the Faculty?

Jim: Yep, yep. I just haven't taken advantage of you, that's all. So

> it's...it's only one person to lay the blame on and that's me. I have...it's down there, it's waiting to go...Steve is willing to help and I've been the oversized elephant with lead in my feet. So it's up to me. It's not your fault or Valerie's or Steve's or the school's or anybody else. It's me. So, we're going to start next week. We're going to make the time.

Quite suddenly the field notes change. In January 1991 for instance:

> I should also note that, during my interview with Jim, he mentioned that it was his birthday, and that he was 51 as of the day of the interview. This had the effect of retroactively explaining a lot of earlier stuff. I had just read an article by Tom Brokaw in *Esquire* about the trauma of turning 50, and it suddenly struck me that, all during the earlier parts of the research project, Jim had been approaching, or living through, the age of 50. His comments about feeling tired, worn out, and old-fashioned suddenly leapt into sharp focus. His generally troubled and distracted air may have something to do with this. And, not least, the fact that he survived his 50th year, and that that particular crisis is now behind him, may have paved the way for him to finally move ahead with a challenging new project which he had been putting off for months.

Other explanations began to emerge:

> Steve then said something that may hold the key to Jim's reluctance to get involved: he said that Jim is a very well-prepared teacher, who always spends a great deal of time getting ready for each class. Steve said that Jim keeps careful records of previous lesson plans and exams, and consults them frequently. He has seen Jim completely replicate a handout for a class by re-

writing it, even though it could be simply reproduced from the older documents.

Meanwhile Jim had begun, in his own time to begin to take up computers - after two years of 'resistance' and as the project had effectively finished. A good job our life history interviews had made us stay with him.

> I started the day in the computer lab, where Jim was once again. While starting later than the others, he seems to be going full steam ahead with the computers. He has had both classes in three times already and has the lab booked for periods 1 and 5 (his two OAC classes) on the following dates: November, 22, 23, 27, 29, 30 and December 3. He was busy printing copies of maps in the lab for use with upcoming projects.

The new sensitivities developed through life history conversations began to emerge in new accounts of the situation:

> Jim, having 'lost his virginity' with the computers, now cannot get enough. He has booked his classes into the lab for 6 of 8 days. To some extent, this appears to be an imitation of Steve's exercise for OAC students. However, I also believe it has to do with the whole rationale for Jim's reluctance to date. He did not want to use the computers just to do some sort of half-assed exercise; if he was going to use them, he wanted it to be a serious data analysis problem. He has now jumped in at the deep end, and is doing a great deal with the system all at once. He is having problems, but coping with them pretty well.

Conclusion

This chapter raises two issues with regard to life history and professional practice: (1) The content issue and (2) The collaboration issue.

Firstly, the paper raises questions about the limits of existing research paradigms to illuminate professional practices. The conventional methods of research observation, structural interviews and surveys are often driven either by researcher perception or practitioner folklore. These are severely circumscribed methods because they fail to engage within the intersection between professional practices and the whole life perspective of professional practitioners. Little attempt is made to explore professional life and work as intersecting with wider whole life perspectives. One researcher on doctors recently explained:

> So much of the work on doctors sees their life only through a professional prism. If they were to see doctors work as primarily viewed as 'an interesting hobby' for middle class men, so much would be viewed differently (Health Researcher, 1998).

Professional work cannot and should not be divorced from the lives of professionals. As can be conclusively evidenced in the example provided, life history studies have the capacity to transform the content of our analyses, of professional practices. Once professional practice is located within a whole life perspective, it has the capacity the *transform* our accounts. The limits of conventional research and accounts are dramatically exposed. In so doing, our research accounts can be dramatically reconceptualised and transformed.

Associated with the re-working of content in the issue of personal voice and perception. In the collaborative life history interview, a reciprocal sharing of views and perceptions takes place. The professional practitioner is empowered to voice a wider range of concerns and to do so as a dialogical exchange which can change both the nature of the account and the nature of consciousness (for both professional and researcher). Our collaborative dialogue has the potential to substantially re-work our understandings of professional practice. Such collaboration can help our studies of professional practice and to do so in ways that illuminate the intersection between life and work. This kind of collaboration is a relatively unexplored modality in studies seeking to reconceptualise our understanding professional practices.

By opening up a dialogue around these issues, the personal voice of the professional is encouraged. The collaboration which underlies life history work opens up a rich flow of dialogue and discussion which can transform our understandings. The example provided in this chapter shows such transformation at work but in a more general sense life history approaches could transform our understandings of the professional and the personal.

There is another sense in which life history approaches can transform the professional paradigms of research. Much research creates a culture of expertise and privilege for the researcher, alongside a culture of silencing, appropriation and academic colonisation, for the researched. Life history seeks, not entirely successfully, to 'level the playing field'.

In some sense, the inequity that is structured into conventional research is destabilised. For the researched are themselves the experts about their own lives; nobody knows better than them the intricacies and intimacies of their life. The researcher, cast into the role of listener, assumes the initial role of learner. From this base, collaboration and analysis follow, but the flow of information and dialogue is partially monitored by those researched. The research trade is, therefore, different to the conventional model. But, of course, with every kind of solution comes new problems. Life history, whilst changing the terms of trade, sets new critical dilemmas. Not least, the access that may be granted to the intimate details of professional life has to be carefully managed in terms of more public reporting and publication.

In summary, life history can transform our accounts and our collaborations. The value and significance of this transformation is substantial. It is well worth further exploration of these methodological approaches, and detailed exploration of the ethical and positional issues that arise in their implementation.

REFERENCES

Goodson, I., & Langsheer, C. (1999). *Computer wars*. New York: St. Martin's Press.

Douglas, C. (1998, June 25). The peoples' frail healer. In *The Guardian*.

Samuel, R. (1989, August 31). Heroes below the hooves of history. In *The Independent*.

Lightning Source UK Ltd.
Milton Keynes UK
06 August 2010

9 789087 904081